TRAUMA
to TRIUMPH

TRAUMA
to TRIUMPH

A Roadmap for Leading Through Disruption
—(and Thriving on the Other Side)—

MARK GOULSTON AND DIANA HENDEL

HARPERCOLLINS
LEADERSHIP

AN IMPRINT OF HARPERCOLLINS

Published by HarperCollins Leadership, an imprint of HarperCollins Focus LLC.

Any internet addresses, phone numbers, or company or product information printed in this book are offered as a resource and are not intended in any way to be or to imply an endorsement by HarperCollins Leadership, nor does HarperCollins Leadership vouch for the existence, content, or services of these sites, phone numbers, companies, or products beyond the life of this book.

ISBN 978-1-4002-2838-6 (eBook)
ISBN 978-1-4002-2837-9 (PBK)

Library of Congress Control Number: 2020952437

Printed in the United States of America
20 21 22 23 LSC 10 9 8 7 6 5 4 3 2 1

CONTENTS

A PERFECT STORM . . . AND A CHAOTIC NEW NORM

WHATEVER YOUR INDUSTRY or role in your organization, there's no denying we are living in a time of incredible upheaval. Multiple events and forces are causing strife in the business world. The chaos we're experiencing now has reached unprecedented levels.

First, of course, is the COVID-19 pandemic. As this book goes to press the virus is still raging across the world. As of mid-November 2020, nearly 11 million have contracted coronavirus and more than 250,000 have died from it in the United States alone. We are leading with COVID-19 because it feels like the epicenter of the quake. Other crises have happened too (and are unfolding as we write these words), and we'll get to those in a moment—but so many of the shakeups feel connected to the COVID-19 pandemic.

The pandemic has disrupted every industry. While some few have thrived (online shopping, digital content providers, grocery stores), others have suffered or are still suffering greatly (airlines, tourism, retail, construction, entertainment). Some of the hardest hit may, eventually, bounce back. There's no way to know for sure. Certainly, many of them will never be the same.

Individual businesses have been impacted in numerous ways. Many had to temporarily close and furlough staff, and in many cases those employees never came back. Revenue is down everywhere. Cash flow shortages create major challenges for business owners. There have also been precipitous drops in customer loyalty, especially for brands not seen as essential. All of these have created major hardships—and in many cases have been fatal for businesses.

In September 2020, CNBC shared some discouraging numbers from Yelp's Economic Impact Report: "As of August 31, 163,735 businesses have indicated on Yelp that they have closed, a 23 percent increase since mid-July. According to Yelp data, permanent closures have reached 97,966, representing 60 percent of closed businesses that won't be reopening."[1]

Global supply chain disruptions have been severe. At the start of the pandemic there was a ripple effect across multiple industries. There were (and continue to be at the time of this writing) shortages of materials. This results in rising costs of supplies and has other negative impacts on businesses. Leaders must figure out how to transform supply chains in a way that reduces uncertainty and makes them more agile and resilient.

Consumer behavior has shifted dramatically. This makes sense when you consider that everything about our way of life has changed, from mandatory masks and social distancing to closures of venues like bars and gyms. In general, people are staying home more than they used to. Naturally all of this changes how people spend money (or don't).

For example (and not surprisingly) folks have turned to online shopping in droves. Plus, for a while there was a decline in discretionary spending, doubtless due both to falling incomes and crippled consumer confidence. When they do leave the house to shop or travel people seem to be sticking very close to home (and favoring companies that show they take safety seriously). They aren't hanging around to browse and thus buy more.

All of this greatly impacts small businesses. The shutdowns dramatically lessened foot traffic, which stores and restaurants count on. What's more, most small businesses run on super-tight margins and can't weather month after month of revenue shortfalls.

Companies have been forced to adapt quickly to consumer behavior changes. They have had to reimagine themselves and their products and make massive changes to their retail environments, their marketing, and more.

For instance, business owners and leaders have suddenly become very aware they must digitally transform in order to serve customers who expect a seamless digital experience. This was already happening, but COVID accelerated it. New consumer behaviors are requiring many businesses to completely overhaul their strategies. None of this is easy.

At the same time all of this has occurred, COVID has transformed the workplace. Think about all that has become routine that could scarcely have been imagined less than a year ago. Masks. Social distancing. New cleaning and sanitation routines. If you still go into an office, a brick and mortar store, or a restaurant (to name just a few) your work life looks very different.

Of course, that's a big *if* since many people are working remotely. If your business is one of the many that have gone virtual, you know the new setup changes the dynamics of interaction between employees and leaders. (Of course, as fate would have it, this massive change is happening when teams most need to up the teamwork and collaboration factors!) So much has to happen virtually and it's a challenge for leaders to create engaging interactions over Zoom.

At the beginning of the pandemic, air travel was severely curtailed. (This is still the case to some extent, though the numbers of people flying have definitely picked up.) What this means for businesses is that conferences and learning have been disrupted. Selling is tougher when it can't happen face to face. It's hard to get dispersed teams together to collaborate. Many people are still afraid to get on a plane and companies are reluctant to insist on it for legal and ethical reasons.

Needless to say, the new way of working is tough on employees. There's a lot of fear and anxiety around catching the virus when people have to come into a physical workplace. Those working remotely often have to deal with issues like homeschooling kids. And even if layoffs haven't directly occurred in an organization, fear of them is palpable among the workforce. All of this can threaten productivity. It also forces leaders to lead in new ways and pay more attention to the mental and emotional health of their employees.

Employers are under pressure to learn all kinds of new things. As mentioned, we've been forced to rethink the way we lead. Also, we've had to master new processes and procedures for keeping employees and customers safe. What do you do when someone in your business gets sick? What are the rules and regulations around the CARES Act and other grants or loans that might be available? Last but not least are the legal obligations. Can you insist employees come to work (or travel) if they are uncomfortable with it? All this is stressful and time-consuming.

All of the changes we've had to navigate since early spring of 2020 are not necessarily *bad*, they're just *different*. Of course change is hard for all of us, but once we get used to a new way of doing things we usually find there are benefits. For example, the expansion of telehealth has potentially increased access to medical professionals for many patients.

We have just spent a lot of time focusing on COVID. That's because in many ways it's the straw that broke the camel's back. Yet that camel was already staggering. There have been, and will continue to be, lots of other big upheavals that create uncertainty for the business world—and, by extension, employees and leaders.

For example, the summer of 2020 ushered in a new focus on racial strife and social justice. Demonstrations broke out across the U.S. following the killing of several Black citizens by members of the police, which sparked riots as communities clashed. And social upheaval doesn't happen in a vacuum. Tensions spill into the workplace, sometimes leading to dissention and divisiveness within the ranks. What's more, all the attention on this issue has created a big push for diversity and inclusion, and leaders are scrambling to make sure they are doing the right things.

Politically, the U.S. has been a powder keg for many years, and will likely continue to be. Racial turmoil, political instability, and changes create a lot of divisiveness, which trickles into the business environment, disrupting relationships. Transfers of power are hard for leaders in other ways, too. In the period leading up to elections there has been lack of clarity around regulatory changes and shifting trade and tax policies. The uncertainty around these issues makes it tough to make long-term strategy decisions.

We've also had our fair share of natural disasters like hurricanes and wildfires. (When writing this book both were happening at the same time—severe flooding on the East Coast and catastrophic fires on the West Coast.) Frighteningly, they're increasing in frequency and severity. It's becoming obvious that so-called "hundred-year events" like storms and floods can happen two years in a row or more often. Worsening weather conditions pose huge challenges to businesses in the danger zone and can devastate supply chains.

We could go on, but we won't. Suffice it to say in a tumultuous world it's impossible to mitigate all the risks.

Stress and chaos are not always the result of terrible disasters. Sometimes positive forces are the culprit. For example, rapid advances in artificial intelligence (AI) and other technology have vastly accelerated the pace of change businesses must deal with. This has been shaking things up for decades. Businesses are forced to constantly learn and upgrade so they can stay relevant. The same phenomenon also displaces employees—new technology makes their jobs obsolete—and forces the remaining ones to learn new skill sets.

All of these crises and changes have created a perfect storm of massive, ongoing upheaval. This is the way we will live going forward: moving from massive change to massive change. Frequency, intensity, and duration have all been ramped up. We are no longer forging through occasional whitewater, but navigating an ongoing VUCA world—one where Volatility, Uncertainty, Complexity, and Ambiguity reign supreme.

A business might be able to weather one crisis, but how can it survive changes that come hard and fast over time? It's a tough question and one that we all have to grapple with sooner or later. (And sooner is better than later.)

Like it or not, we all exist in a state of flux. We must be able to pivot to meet rapidly changing needs, while not losing sight of the long view.

All of this means we must create a culture where people have the skillset that allows them to navigate the next major disruption, the next pandemic . . . or natural disaster . . . or trade war . . . or cybersecurity attack. It will always be something.

That's why the message of this book is so important. As the external environment continues to shift, leaders will need to understand what is happening, how it impacts every member of the team (including themselves), and what they need to do about it. Your very survival depends on realizing that we've moved beyond stress and are now in trauma territory.

That realization will change everything for you. It will set you up to put a blueprint in place—one you can follow through every huge crisis, minor disaster, and "challenge" that comes your way in our new normal. You'll be able to shore up some foundational principles that are paramount for meeting head-on what the future throws at you. And you'll get better and better at managing the constant change that now defines our world.

It is urgent that we take action, not tomorrow, but now. We need to look back on this time as a turning point. Not only did we face trauma, we successfully navigated it and came out stronger, smarter, tougher, and better than before.

/ PART 1 /

UNDERSTANDING THE IMPACT OF TRAUMA

BEFORE YOU CAN SUCCESSFULLY NAVIGATE A TRAUMATIC CRISIS and use it as a springboard to becoming a stronger organization, you must adjust your mindset. First, you must become aware that what people are experiencing *is* trauma, and *not just* typical workplace stress. And second, you must realize that unprocessed, un-dealt-with trauma is extremely damaging to your organization. Only after you accept these two premises will you be likely to take the most effective actions.

You've probably heard the Nietzsche quote "That which does not kill us makes us stronger." To an extent, we agree: Going through trauma *can* make an organization stronger. Trauma can be a growth experience. But if we don't handle a traumatic crisis effectively, it will, instead, make us *weaker*—and in a hyper-competitive marketplace few organizations can afford to operate at a less than optimal level of performance.

In the next few chapters we'll explain exactly what trauma looks like inside an organization and how deep the damage can go.

First, you'll learn why trauma is so pervasive these days. The tremendous chaos we're collectively experiencing (as described in the introduction) means that many organizations have moved past stress and into trauma.

Next, Diana will share her own story of surviving a deadly workplace shooting as a case study. She'll lay out some common threads connecting what happened in the wake of this horrific act of violence to the impacts of other (typically perceived as "lesser") disruptive events. The point? Trauma is trauma, whatever it looks like, and it's all destructive.

Then, we'll go into more detail on how trauma impacts individuals and disrupts organizations that haven't adequately prepared for such crises. Part 1 culminates in a chapter exploring how trauma sparks division inside organizations, polarizes them, and can create a pendulum swing between extreme solutions. (To help you better understand, we also explore how this polarization is playing out on a national level with COVID-19.)

We hope that what you learn in the first part of this book will set your resolve to start creating the roadmap we describe in Part 2. Thank you for reading, and we wish you the best of luck as you set off on a journey that will, hopefully, help you not just survive current and future traumas but actually thrive in their aftermath.

CHAPTER 1

WE'VE MOVED FROM STRESS TO TRAUMA— AND THAT CHANGES EVERYTHING

IN THE INTRODUCTION, we took a look at all the factors swirling around and whipping up chaos in our external environment. No doubt the pressures leaders and employees face and the changes we must navigate are incredibly stressful. But to assume that what we're dealing with is only stress is a dangerous misconception. Due to the frequency, intensity, and duration of the crises and changes we are experiencing, we've moved beyond stress and crossed into trauma territory.

Trauma is different from stress. While stress upsets our balance in the moment, we still maintain a feeling of control over our lives. Most of us deal with routine stress daily and are able to manage it (up to a point, anyway). Trauma, on the other hand, overwhelms our self-protective structure and sends us scrambling for survival. It leaves us vulnerable, helpless, groundless. It shatters our sense of safety and security and changes how we look at the world. And unaddressed, it can result in long-term harm.

▪ ▪ ▪

DIFFERENT TYPES OF TRAUMA

If you haven't experienced a traumatic crisis yet, you almost certainly will. It is estimated that 70 percent of people in the U.S. will experience at least one traumatic event in their lives.[1] Yet trauma doesn't always look like you might expect.

Sure, sometimes trauma is a sudden single event: a shocking act of violence, or a terrible workplace accident that leads to severe injury or death, or a suicide. It may be an act of fraud or embezzlement perpetrated by a leader that threatens everyone with disgrace and financial ruin.

These kinds of acute trauma are easy to see. Leaders may assume that because these kinds of "shock and awe" events are rare and unlikely, it's not as urgent to learn about their potential impact. But when you consider that there's another type of trauma, one that's far more prevalent, you'll see why this subject is so crucial.

Sometimes trauma is ongoing and cumulative. For example, it may take the form of sexual harassment, or racism, or discrimination. When trauma is not connected to a single event, many of us may not even realize we're experiencing its effects. In these kinds of scenarios, where the trauma is chronic and perhaps not visible to the whole organization, the organization is like the proverbial frog in the cooking pot. You know the story: At first the frog is sitting in lukewarm water. Over time, the heat slowing intensifies until, finally, it is at the boiling point and the frog is in serious trouble.

A third type of trauma—complex trauma—comes from exposure to multiple traumatic events. While this would seem to be rare, in our increasingly complex and chaotic world, it's on the increase.

However trauma manifests—a sudden, shocking event or a sneaky process that slowly unfolds, or the confluence of several different ones—it *will* have a destructive impact. When employees experience trauma, they start acting from a place of fear. They are in survival mode, caught up in the "flight, fight, or freeze" response. (To leaders their behavior may look like stubbornness, belligerence, aggression, avoidance, or other types of "difficult" behavior.)

And when *everyone* is in the grip of trauma, it is deeply destructive to your organization. Your leaders and employees will suffer. Your structures, systems, and values will be compromised. Trauma will change the way you function. Thus, it makes sense to prepare for trauma (if it hasn't yet occurred) or deal with it quickly and decisively (if it has).

But few of us know how to effectively navigate the emotions that arise from trauma and its long-term impacts. As leaders, we need to learn how to effectively address trauma, so that we can help people move productively through it and thrive in the aftermath. If we try to simply treat trauma in ourselves and our employees the same way we have treated stress in the past, we will fall short. At best, recovery will be slow and incomplete—if the business survives long enough for it to take place at all.

Here's the point: Leading people through a traumatic crisis is a different ballgame. It's not enough to help them master coping skills and build up resilience. That works for stress. Those tactics, alone, are insufficient, though, to address the effects of trauma. Leading people through trauma is partly about helping them heal, but just as important, it's about creating stability in the midst of chaos, minimizing the negative effects of trauma (and capitalizing on the positive ones that emerge), and creating a path toward a thriving future. All of this can only help you and your organization deal better with the next crisis that hits.

COVID-19 IS TURNING UP THE HEAT

In a very real way, we're all struggling with "collective" trauma brought on by COVID-19. The pandemic has wreaked havoc on both individuals and on our nation as a whole. Millions of people have become infected or have had loved ones get sick or die. Some have lost their jobs, some their businesses. Almost all of us have lost our previous feelings of freedom to travel and to engage with others. For nearly everyone, the pandemic has and will continue to disrupt our lives.

Of course, organizations have been impacted—some more severely than others. Almost every day, we are in contact with leaders whose organizations continue to deal with the traumatic fallout. Overnight, these leaders faced chaos and confusion, as they found themselves in survival mode with little concrete information, struggling to react swiftly and decisively to ensure the safety of employees, coordinate response plans, and effectively communicate with their workforce.

Many have learned valuable lessons in response to the pandemic—and though they made mistakes early on, they did many things remarkably well. In some instances, it has brought out the best of them in terms of camaraderie, innovation, speed, and agility. Many are intentionally reevaluating their operations, and, in particular, their rapid response processes, communication strategies, teambuilding, and decision-making structures, to ensure that they not only navigate future traumas more successfully, but also thrive in the aftermath.

Right now, you may be thinking *There's nothing I could have done to prepare for COVID-19 and its impact.* This is not true. Certainly, you couldn't have known the specifics. But there are (surprisingly effective) ways to prepare for unknown crises. And the first step is to bring the subject of organizational trauma out of the closet.

WE MUST "NAME, FRAME, AND CLAIM" TRAUMA

Only when we address trauma as trauma will we be able to move forward. Naming, claiming, and framing trauma helps us understand what is happening to individuals and to the group. It gives us the language to talk about it so that everyone is on the same page. It helps people understand "This is why I am feeling so bad!" And it gives everyone permission to finally seek real help.

There's a saying that if we don't deal with our crap, our crap deals with us. If we don't deal with trauma—and its impact on individuals and on our organizations as a whole—we effectively risk "normalizing" this state of being. It's like we've been in an accident and have broken both legs but rather than seeking medical attention and getting the bones set, we just accept that for the rest of our life we're going to limp along on crutches.

Sadly, many organizations *do* accept a traumatized workforce as normal. Perhaps leaders don't recognize the impairment that has happened. Or they've been traumatized themselves. (Often when trauma patterns are well-established and we've worked inside them for years, we can't see the forest for the trees.) Many may feel that something is off but have no idea how to deal with it. And so, they don't.

This brings us to the biggest reason to name, frame, and claim trauma: It sets you up to prepare for future disruptive events. When you know what causes trauma and what it looks like, you can stave off its most devastating impacts. You can better understand your employees and respond to them from a place of empathy, with methods that really work. You can avoid mistakes and reduce piling on even more stress in an already tough time.

Best of all, you can create a blueprint to follow again and again as you navigate the perfect storm of uncertainty and upheaval that is today's business world. We may never have another pandemic. (Let's hope not!) But change will never cease. We owe it to ourselves, our employees, and our organizations to manage it in any form it takes.

In the next chapter, Diana will share her own trauma story. Fair warning: It's intense and upsetting. But we think it will go a long way toward helping you understand why we care so much about the subject of organizational trauma. And it will show you by example what you can expect to happen when trauma hits home. That, in turn, will set you up to learn how to navigate it and come out stronger on the other side.

CHAPTER 2

DIANA'S STORY: A CASE STUDY

BEFORE AND AFTER

Though April 16, 2009, began much like any other, the date came to mark a definitive "before" and "after" in my life and in the lives of many others. What occurred on that day, and followed in the aftermath, tested all that I had believed about leadership, redefined what it meant to lead through crisis, and even changed the way I led in routine, everyday circumstances thereafter.

I had started the day early by rounding, coffee in hand, through the halls of the hospital where I served as the CEO. I greeted visitors and patients and stopped to chat with employees and doctors.

Rounding was one of my favorite administrative activities: It was a great way to both directly connect with my colleagues and informally assess the current mood of the organization.

That morning I'd sensed an overall lightheartedness in the air, an easing up, that replaced a previous pall of uncertainty and apprehension.

We were in the midst of a difficult budget season which, combined with the financial crash of 2008, had contributed to an atmosphere of stress and worry that had hung over the organization—and the entire community—for the past several months. Though we'd recently had a small layoff, our financials had begun to turn the corner and newly released reports indicated our bottom line had improved substantially. I was relieved and also hopeful that more reductions in our workforce would not be needed. Perhaps the lightheartedness hinted at a return to normalcy and stability, I thought. Or perhaps I was just projecting my own, newly buoyant, increasingly optimistic state of mind.

Later, I would attribute the good feelings of that morning—in the "before times"—to innocence: the innocence of not knowing what the day had in store for us. I had no way of knowing that I was about to be part of a traumatic experience that would change how I saw myself as a leader and alter my vision of the future. Yet while viewing that day through the lens of hindsight makes me wish to reverse time, it also brings into sharp relief the recognition that our process of repairing, healing, and renewal had been profoundly galvanizing, unifying, and ultimately, transformational, too. I learned that I could lead in a way that would both optimize our ability to respond to any future disruption *and* maximize our ability to thrive in its aftermath.

But before I tell you more about the trauma that led to this new way of leading and sparked the development of the roadmap in this book, let me start first by sharing a little about my professional background and the organization I worked in for nearly twenty-seven years.

A CITY WITHIN A CITY

For more than a century, Memorial Hospital has served the diverse, densely populated community of greater Long Beach, California. Home to two large, not-for-profit teaching hospitals—one catering to the healthcare needs of adults and the other to the unique needs of children—the fifty-four-acre campus is one of the biggest and busiest medical center complexes on the West Coast. With nearly $1 billion in annual revenues, more than 6,000 employees, and 1,500 independent physicians and specialists, the hospitals are a major economic engine in a region with a population of more than a million.

It is a city within a city. Words like *legacy* and *cornerstone* and *premiere* describe it.

From a career perspective, I had grown up in the organization. I had arrived in 1988 as an eager pharmacy student, hoping to secure a permanent position. And when I did, I was hooked. I'd known then that I intended to spend my entire career in the organization. Over the next twenty years, I was progressively promoted throughout the larger health system to bigger leadership roles with more and more responsibility. In early 2009, I became the hospitals' CEO.

I was part of a tribe, a team of people dedicated to caring for others across the entire spectrum of their lives, literally from birth to death. We welcomed new life. We treated, healed, and saved lives. And we eased lives as they faded and passed. We were a community of caregivers who were there for people on the best and the worst days of their lives. We were a safe haven, a sanctuary for patients coming to us with illnesses and injuries from the outside world.

Our workforce was a cross-sectional representation of our community—demographically, sociologically, and personality-wise. In our long history together, strong allegiances and loyalties had been developed within and between departments and units, often crossing generations, functional roles, and traditional hierarchies. Our workplace was a complex mosaic of affiliations and identities, united by meaning, a shared purpose and shared experiences, and a strong sense of belonging.

But the "shadow" sides to our cultural strengths—conflict, communication breakdowns, betrayals, siloes, strikes, burnout, and confusion (and all the other kinds of things you have seen on *ER* or *Grey's Anatomy*)—were also present. In short, we were members of a family with all its joys and wonders—and its dysfunctions.

TRAUMA HITS HOME

Throughout my career I'd had numerous encounters with adversity and a lot of experience managing the unexpected, from operational mishaps to financial hardship to internal and external disasters to minor scandals and PR nightmares. Our teams and I had been well-trained and seasoned in crisis management—after all, trauma was a big part of our business—but it was almost always *other* people's traumas we faced. That changed on April 16, 2009.

On that day a man entered the outpatient pharmacy of the hospital, which was adjacent to the main lobby, and shot the supervisor several times at point blank range. He then ran a considerable distance through the medical center and then onto a street outside the emergency department, where he encountered the executive director of the pharmacy department and shot him several times, before turning the gun on himself. All three died on site.

Obviously, this event was terrifying for those who witnessed the shootings and responded to the scenes. But regardless of proximity or involvement, it was traumatic for everyone in the organization—because the shooter was an insider. Not only was he a member of our staff, he was beloved by many and had been recently honored as an employee of the month. A highly regarded, award-winning colleague had come to work and shot and killed his bosses.

This shooting was not an accident, a random act, or an impulsive crime of passion. It wasn't a mishap, or a case of the victims being in the wrong place at the wrong time. It was premeditated and planned and the shooter had the presence of mind to move from one scene to another, addressing many co-workers by name as he passed them in the hallways, telling them to get out of the way, that he didn't want to hurt them. He had specifically targeted his two bosses.

As an acute care hospital, we couldn't close after the shooting or stop to regroup. We still had more than six hundred patients in-house who needed our care. Like the oft-cited business idiom, we had to continue flying the plane and repair it at the same time. In our version, we were continuing to fly a plane full of passengers, while repairing a gaping hole in the fuselage.

Though we made mistakes, we also did a good job in many ways of managing the event and its immediate aftermath. The structure of a familiar and well-practiced "incident command system" provided focus and direction, kept us aligned toward common goals, and helped to steady our emotions. Our coordinated response exposed our connectedness and camaraderie, and revealed an extraordinary esprit de corps. In survival mode, many positives were evident, driven primarily around our human tendency, at least initially, to come together in a crisis.

But even when the immediate danger had passed and the event was deemed "over," the full extent of its impact didn't end on the day of the shooting. Many individuals—and the organization itself—had been severely traumatized and shaken to the core. And it didn't take long for blame, guilt, shame, and fear to emerge from the shadows and for the event to become difficult and painful to talk about, bordering on taboo.

THE AFTERMATH

A new threat to the organization and its cultural well-being emerged almost immediately following the shooting: the quest for the motive. While facts surrounding the shooting were slow to emerge, speculation about *why* it happened sprung up instantly. The question (so familiar to anyone in grief) exposed our fundamentally human need to know the cause or have a reason for why a bad thing has happened. Logically, we think that if we have an answer, we can then *do something* to regain our sense of safety and security and restore order and certainty to our lives.

And while we all might have believed that knowing *why* would quell the feelings of loss of control and helplessness and diminish fear of the unknown, the search for it might also inflict far-reaching and long-lasting harm. Rumors about the motive were loaded with the potential to pit employees and managers against one another, sow distrust, and heighten our collective fear. I worried that the rumors would create deep division between us and rip our organization apart.

Though we had shared a traumatic experience, we'd each experienced it differently. We'd also had our own relationships with the victims and the shooter. As a result, there were thousands of unique points of view about what had happened and why it had happened. To make sense of it, each of us created a narrative based on our own perspectives and personal histories. Some had lots of facts about the event; some had few. Some people had known the shooter well; some, not at all. Some of us had been close to the victims. Some had never met them. And though very few of us had access to the facts and details, nearly everyone had an opinion about the shooter's state of mind.

Those further removed seemed to find it easier to make sweeping generalizations about the motive. Some held the organization, the recession, the recent or impending layoffs, or others responsible. Some simply proclaimed that the shooter had been deranged, because only a deranged person would shoot people. Most assigned blame solely to the shooter himself. But some of us would struggle with that.

The long list of motives that were churned up cast a wide net of secondary blame. Why hadn't we prevented it or stopped it? Did we cause it, provoke it, or allow it? We did a lot of second-guessing. How had we not seen it coming? Had our background checks failed us? Should there have been bulletproof glass in the pharmacy? Should the security guards have been armed?

A MORASS OF SHAME, BLAME, AND GUILT

Understandably, those closest to the trauma would not only be caught in a web of self-blame, but also wracked with guilt. For me, the rumored motive related to layoffs remained stubbornly lodged in my mind. I felt guilty about the layoff itself, and guilt for surviving while my colleagues did not. Knowing it was irrational and misattributed didn't convince me otherwise. Trauma has a way of injecting guilt into those closest to it, or those most affected by it.

Over time, it became apparent to me that others also harbored survivor's guilt and self-blame. They searched their memories, tormenting themselves with the trauma-induced magical thinking that they'd somehow caused or contributed to the tragedy. Had a complaint or a grievance they'd shared with the shooter somehow prodded him into action? Had they missed a sign? Could they have stopped it? They wondered how a person they regarded as a good, trusted friend could do something so awful. They doubted their own judgments.

And though guilt and blame had major repercussions for individuals and the organization as a whole, simply believing that he didn't have a distinct motive—and that he must have been just evil or crazy—didn't provide much of a sense of safety, either. The shooting had shattered the belief that we were in one of the safest, most-trusted environments possible. Who else among us might suddenly snap? Were there accomplices? Were managers being targeted? On an individual level, the experience of the trauma had unleased a cascade of normal biological reactions—"fight, flight, and freeze"—and put our nervous systems on high alert.

We didn't want the shooting to define us, but a feeling of shame arose that begged the question that perhaps it, instead, described us. The shooter had been one of us, and we'd recently honored him as an employee of the month. What had our culture fostered? How could our patients trust our judgment? How could the public trust us in the aftermath? None of us wanted to become known as "that hospital where an employee murdered his bosses."

Talking about the tragedy was key to our recovery, but it also presented a dilemma: How much should be shared and what words should be used? The first tests of communication had already occurred. We'd checked all the boxes on our disaster plan communication template—press conferences, email updates, webcast, town halls, rounding, etc. But this wasn't just a scandal or a crisis or reporting on a turn of events. It was far more complicated and delicate, and a fine line existed between transparency and confidentiality.

THE PATH TO UNSPEAKABILITY

In retrospect I realize that being able to talk openly about these negative perceptions of our culture might have dispelled myths or prevented false narratives from filling the void. It might have kept them from becoming confused with truth simply because they were so strongly felt. And it might have kept us from carrying blame and guilt and shame as silent passengers. But it had been too sensitive a subject—too emotionally and politically risky—to talk about. It hadn't felt safe to ask questions we didn't know—or were afraid to know—the answers to. We weren't capable—I wasn't capable—of leading frank discussions about the shadow sides of our culture. Not when the shadows were that dark.

Soon the shooting became an unspeakable topic. But it didn't mean it had gone away. It lingered and hovered, phantom-like, among our everyday operations. Once the memorial services were over, there was no ongoing way to honor the victims, or to collectively acknowledge our feelings, and yet we showed up to work every day in the same location where the tragedy had occurred.

We had all hoped that the formal homicide investigation would eventually reveal a clear-cut answer that alleviated our feelings of guilt and blame and simultaneously restored our sense of safety. That didn't happen. In the end, the report was inconclusive. No definitive motive was found, leaving us with mystery and the disconcerting knowledge that we would never know *why*. On the one hand, it eliminated overt and public finger-pointing, but, on the other, left us each privately unresolved and alone with our own traumatically forged narratives.

All of this, in the long run, caused both negative consequences for many individuals and for the organization as a whole—and, unexpectedly, many positive ones as well. We wouldn't be able to go completely back to business-as-usual, back to how it had been "before." But, we also knew we'd have to resist the forces of division and become unified if we had any chance of repairing and healing. We could not turn on one another. We would need to draw on our strength, reflecting every bit of goodness and compassion and empathy we'd ever felt toward one another. We could not forget that we were collectively part of something much larger than ourselves.

EMERGING FROM THE DARKNESS

Though trauma had caused long-lasting damage, survivorship presented us with the opportunity to establish new models for leading and managing in the future and motivated us to intentionally change in ways we hadn't considered in the past.

In the year that followed, the organization rebounded, moved on, and, in many ways, grew stronger than it had been before.

We developed newfound appreciation and respect for one another. Through our collective experience, our commitment to purpose and meaning was reinforced. In many ways, we became more tightly bound together than we had ever been before. Our communication philosophies and practices, teambuilding and succession-planning activities, and decision-making processes were transformed. All this, ultimately, made us not only better prepared to deal with future traumas (we came to realize that it was not a matter of if, but when), but also enabled us to perform better in routine, everyday situations thereafter.

An air of optimism and enthusiasm permeated the organization. Yes, we had setbacks and failures, and there were cracks in our renewed unity, but overall, we'd rebounded stronger than ever. We had beaten the odds and spiraled upward after the trauma. I was proud of our team's—and my own—resolve to move forward and not allow it to divide us or hold us back.

But sadly, one-by-one, many of those who had been directly traumatized by the shooting began to leave. With each departure, there were a few sympathetic murmurs but little discussion. The topic was still unspeakable. I began to wonder if I'd someday hear myself say, "And then there were none."

Still, I was convinced that I would never need to leave prematurely because I had successfully transitioned to leading us in the "new normal." I had never been more professionally fulfilled, nor more certain I was right where I belonged. I was in it for the long haul. And I believed my emotional wounds from the shooting could be completely healed by continuing to manifest the deep meaning I'd found in my work. Surely, the strong alignment of my own calling with the organization's mission would continue to propel me forward into the future.

TOUGHNESS AND BUSYNESS ARE NO ANTIDOTE

That's what I thought at the time. But I was wrong. For years after the shooting I coped, mostly in positive and socially acceptable ways. I thought I was immune to PTSD: I'd been through crises and disasters and was mentally tough. Toughness wasn't the antidote, however. Nor was busyness (though for a while it kept my symptoms away). Over the years, my hypervigilance and isolation increased, which led, increasingly, to anxiety and depression.

Eventually all this culminated in a diagnosis of PTSD, which ultimately ended my career as I'd known it. Six years after the shooting, and with a strong team in place, I decided to step aside. The organization deserved a healthy leader and I deserved to fully recover and heal.

Fortunately, with the help of experts and a lot of hard work, I was able to fully process the trauma and completely recover. And I rebounded career-wise. In the years that followed, I launched an executive coaching and consulting practice and published a memoir, *Responsible*, about the impact of the trauma on me as a leader and on the culture of an organization. I also began speaking to groups about leading through trauma and sharing the best practices I'd learned through my own direct experience, my work consulting with other organizations that had been traumatized, and as a member of a small but growing network of organizational trauma experts.

From an extensive study of the available literature, I discovered that while a lot had been written about the impact of trauma on individuals, very little had been published to help leaders and their teams specifically navigate the effects of trauma on the organization itself. Studying and reporting on "organizational trauma" is still relatively new territory. (Pat Vivian and Shana Hormann, PhD, MSW, authors of *Organizational Trauma and Healing*, were among the first to coin the term.)

And though my story of the shooting that I've just shared with you is an extreme example of organizational trauma (and at first, might seem rare and unrelatable), as I shared it with other leaders, it quickly became clear that there were many parallels and common characteristics to what they had experienced when traumas occurred in their workplaces.

COMMON THREADS OF TRAUMA

As word spread and my practice grew, I began to get calls for help from leaders whose organizations were in the throes, or in the aftermath, of a major disruptive event. Most didn't call it "trauma," but it quickly became obvious that what they described was an organization that had been traumatized. Though most had been accustomed to managing crisis or scandal, many reported that the effects of the event had continued to persist far longer than expected.

All said that their organizations were struggling to move on and indicated that, at least on some level, distrust, uncertainty, lack of safety (psychological and/or physical), blame, guilt, and internal division were preventing them from full closure and healing. Most also reported a lasting feeling of shame—and that the internal reputation of the organization had been harmed. They worried about the potential for it to be damaged externally as well.

Increasingly, I encountered real-time scenarios and heard stories from the past of how a variety of traumas—sexual harassment, the sudden death of a co-worker, a natural disaster, threats of violence, and mass layoffs (or the ongoing threat of them)—had not just affected individuals, but had also affected the organization itself, by challenging or shattering people's beliefs about its culture, sowing distrust and lack of confidence, and damaging its reputation. All of these factors hampered the organization's ability to thrive (and in a couple of cases, function).

Here are some of the common threads that I see in traumatized organizations:

- **Communication falters.** Frequently, communication is initially haphazard and often too little and too late as leaders struggle to navigate the line between transparency and confidentiality. Trust and confidence quickly erode as wild rumors spread and strong opinions surface. It's unclear how decisions will be made (and who is responsible for making them).
- **People create their own narratives.** There are hundreds of unique points of view, and each person creates a narrative based on their own perspectives, personal histories, and relationships to those directly involved.
- **Blaming and finger-pointing ensue.** Speculation and second-guessing can cast a wide net of secondary blame that extends well beyond the perpetrator or causal agent. Why didn't the organization prevent it or stop it? How could the leaders have been unaware? In some instances, people blame the victims for overreacting, or the organization for not preventing "witch hunts."
- **Feelings of guilt rise to the surface.** Those closest to a traumatic event may struggle with feelings of guilt: guilt that they'd missed a sign, hadn't stopped it from happening, or hadn't spoken up sooner—and that it had then happened to others. Some feel guilty for surviving.
- **The workforce rapidly polarizes.** People tend to divide into opposing factions. For example, in one organization that experienced a sexual harassment case, "Camp 1" believed and sided with the victims while "Camp 2" defended the accused.
- **A sense of shame arises.** People often worry that the traumatic event (a shooting, a rape, a financial scandal) will

define them. They may feel ashamed that their culture could give rise to such an event. If the event is covered in the media, that shame deepens. They wonder: Will others—staff members, customers, the community—ever trust the organization again?

- **Trauma becomes unspeakable.** Often a trauma grows exceedingly difficult and painful to talk about—bordering on taboo—and becomes "unspeakable." Because it isn't being addressed, people continue to struggle and the ongoing, perhaps deepening of division/polarization, blame, shame, and guilt hurts the culture. All of this can damage collaboration, cooperation, cohesiveness, and teamwork and erode people's belief and trust in one another.

Without intervention, the repercussions of trauma can be long-lasting and increasingly destructive. However—and I've seen this again and again—seeking help changes everything. This means helping the individuals directly impacted by the trauma and also addressing the damage that's been done to the organization as a whole.

With a thoughtful and timely response, it's quite possible to turn trauma into triumph. Not only can you successfully reunify and recover but you can emerge with a culture that is stronger, more transparent, and better able to intervene and handle any disruption in the future.

NOW IS THE TIME TO BREAK THE TRAUMA CYCLE

As mentioned earlier, the field of organizational trauma is a very new one. A good amount has been written on how trauma affects individuals, but most people don't realize how much lasting impact a traumatic event can have on an organization's culture. The good news is that the effects of trauma are becoming more widely understood. We learn more and more every day.

Our hope is that this book will help fill in the gaps in understanding and create a sense of urgency in leaders to act quickly to break the cycle set in motion by trauma. We want to give a practical, readable, actionable guide that explains without overwhelming and is oriented toward solutions.

In the following chapters, you will learn how trauma manifests in individuals and, collectively, in organizations. You'll discover how it can polarize and divide, often causing false choices to emerge or exposing ones that already exist but had not been previously recognized. In almost all cases, organizations initially are focused on survival. Some take actions to ensure survival in the short run, but which may hinder their ability to thrive in the long run. Others take actions in hopes of surviving in the long run, but which greatly harm their prospects in the short run. Often, this is a false choice and leads an organization to swing back and forth between one pole and the other.

And, of course, you'll learn how to better deal with traumatic crisis: how to establish processes that help your organization navigate the immediate effects of a trauma, how to communicate in times of trauma, how to redesign decision-making processes, and how to create a roadmap to guide you in the future—both in the short-term and in the long-term. The truth is, individuals and companies can grow and thrive in the aftermath of trauma.

We hope this book will show you the benefits of preparing for trauma before it hits. When you have a plan in place—one that encompasses tools, processes, and systems to use in the immediate aftermath of crisis as well as in the longer term—you can spare yourself many costly mistakes. You can reduce stress—your own and your employees'—when everyone is on the same page and knows what to expect and what actions to take. Having a plan will help you to respond calmly and steadily in the midst of chaos. You'll make better decisions. If you wait until trauma hits to create this plan, it will be a lot harder to do.

Finally, we hope you'll see this book as a blueprint for managing change in general. We live in a time of constant flux and chaos. Even if a major traumatic crisis never hits your company, you'll certainly experience minor emergencies and periods of intense change. The tools you're about to learn will help to navigate all of them.

Once you understand the dynamics of trauma, you'll be better equipped to lead your company through any kind of disruption and come out stronger, better, and more aligned and unified on the other side. Let's get started!

CHAPTER 3

THE EFFECTS OF TRAUMA ON INDIVIDUALS

EADERS MUST BE able to lead in two ways. They must lead individuals and organizations. These are two very different (yet intertwined) skillsets. Leading individual employees is about engaging, motivating, giving good feedback, and so forth. It's also about understanding that everyone is unique: Everything from age to gender to race to family status to religious belief to political leanings to plain-old human biases and preferences impacts how each of us show up at work.

Leading organizations is about creating a vision, strategic goal-setting, making decisions, prioritizing tasks, etc. . . . but it's *also* about understanding, anticipating, and shaping group dynamics. In an organization people are not just individuals but part of a collective. Their behavior "shape shifts" in response to the behavior of those around them.

Likewise, when trauma occurs, it impacts your company on two levels: the individual level and the organizational level. Leaders must be able to understand and respond to trauma in both contexts. In this chapter we will be looking at the effects of trauma on individuals. In the next, we will learn about trauma from an organizational perspective.

Keep in mind that when we talk about trauma and individuals, we aren't just referring to employees. We also mean leaders. Every leader in your organization—from CEO to middle manager to frontline supervisor—is subject to the effects of trauma. You might think leaders just "know what to do" when trauma occurs, but they, too (meaning you, too) are struggling with the same issues as everyone else.

REMINDER: ROUTINE STRESS AND TRAUMATIC STRESS ARE DIFFERENT

We have already established that traumatic stress in the workplace is different than work-related stress.

In our book *Why Cope When You Can Heal?* we describe trauma as a deeply distressing, disturbing, and overwhelming event that often involves death, destruction, or severe disruption (or the threat of it). It is often something unexpected that catches someone by surprise, and causes them to feel fear, horror, and lack of control. Trauma overwhelms the self-protective structure and leaves people feeling vulnerable and helpless. When trauma occurs, their priority centers on immediate safety and security—on survival. Experiencing trauma can shatter their previous sense of safety and security. It can change the way they look at the world. And it can create lasting harm.

Let's take a quick look the biological realities of trauma.

WHAT'S HAPPENING ON THE INSIDE: THE PHYSIOLOGICAL AND PSYCHOLOGICAL IMPACT OF TRAUMA

When a person is traumatized, an involuntary and automatic biological and psychological survival mechanism is unleashed: the *fight, flight, freeze* response. As human beings we simply can't avoid survival mechanisms. Nor would we want to. After all, there are more unknowns in life than knowns. If we were unfazed by these unknowns, or underestimate their possible impact, the results could be catastrophic. Without our ancestors' fight, flight, freeze response we most likely wouldn't be here.

Simply put, the fight, flight, freeze response is the body's natural response to danger. Fight and flight enable us to either defend ourselves or flee to safety when a threat arises. The freeze response—which is less widely known—is another means of survival. During the freeze response, we freeze as a means of survival—much like playing dead in the animal kingdom.

Experiencing a trauma leads to a large release of cortisol, a stress hormone, from your adrenal glands that helps the body get physically ready for what's ahead. Cortisol also sends a signal to a part of the brain called the amygdala that says, "forget about thinking, let's survive." Blood rushes to your survival brain, along with adrenaline to help you survive whatever comes next.

This is when the "amygdala hijack" occurs. The amygdala is located in our middle/mammalian/emotional brain. When we are triggered by a traumatizing event our elevated cortisol signals the amygdala part of our brain (our "emotional sentinel") to divert blood away from our upper, rational thinking brain to our lower, survival brain. In this moment our choices are fear, panic, paralysis *or* anger, hostility, and attack. There's no middle ground. Trauma triggers this intense fear and when we feel cornered our choice is to attack (fight), run (flight), or be immobilized (freeze).

Keep in mind that responses to trauma may vary wildly from person to person. An individual's response is what the body/nervous system instantly determines is best to survive a trauma or threat. It's not a conscious decision, but an automatic and involuntary response that happens in a split second and that is based on a conditioned reflex. This means that in any given situation, one person may react with fighting, while another reacts with fleeing or freezing. So, in any shared trauma, one individual could easily have different reactions (based on proximity, what they observe, what they hear, as well as on their unique background and experience) from those of another nearby person.

The good news is that after an acute stress response the nervous system usually resets itself once the immediate danger has passed and goes back to its pre-trauma functioning. But sometimes, and understandably if trauma is ongoing, chronic, and unrelenting (like the COVID-19 pandemic), it can lead to ongoing anxiety, fear, shock, numbness that lasts much longer. People may start to notice an increased startle response and symptoms such as insomnia nightmares, and/or flashbacks.

FLIGHT, FRIGHT, FREEZE, FRIEND: INTRODUCING THE FOURTH F

If you're like most readers you've most likely heard or read about some of this fight/flight/freeze stuff before. However, you may not have heard about the fourth "F" that occurs in response to trauma: *friend*. This "F" represents the bonding that occurs in response to trauma due to the presence of oxytocin (the "love" hormone that fuels friendships).

When people feel bonded with others the oxytocin counteracts high cortisol levels and can prevent or stop an amygdala hijack. Blood returns to your upper brain so you can think again. Dopamine also increases. These two hormones give you a sense of relief and then pleasure, both of which can at least temporarily mitigate the effects of fear.

If leaders can leverage the camaraderie created by the fourth F early on to bring the entire organization together, it can reduce the formation of rigid factions as individuals take sides and develop various narratives surrounding the trauma. Left unchecked, the division that results can be toxic and may further cripple the organization. (We discuss this further in upcoming chapters.)

WHAT TRAUMA LOOKS LIKE FROM THE OUTSIDE (A FEW RED FLAGS)

With all of this hormonal drama going on inside your employees' brains, you might think it would be obvious that people are traumatized. This is not always the case. For one thing, the effects of trauma aren't always visible. While it's possible for a person struggling with trauma to shake, sweat, cry, appear terrified, or show other outward signs, it's also common for them to look and behave the same as anyone else—especially when they have their "game faces" on for work. This does not mean that they are not suffering or that trauma will not break through later.

What's more, when traumatized people do "act out" in various ways, leaders rarely recognize their behavior for what it is. To a leader, an employee struggling with ongoing traumatic stress may simply come off as angry or hostile or distant. Also leaders who feel out of their area of competence to handle the internal emotions of an employee may indirectly encourage a "don't ask, don't tell" atmosphere, that can increase the level of trauma that individual is feeling. The truth is, many remain in the grip of fear. They unconsciously or consciously may believe that whatever comes next will kill them. The employees' behaviors (especially if they're markedly different—negative *and* positive changes—from how they normally act) may be a manifestation of trauma.

Here are some red flags that individuals in your organization might be suffering from trauma:

People cling to their "Competence Zone." They may rigidly cling to what has worked for them in the past. "This is where I'm competent. This is where I'm confident. This is where I feel in control." They may blindly keep doing what they've always done, even though it no longer works—or even though their skillset is in less demand than it used to be, due to the pace of change around them.

When asked to change, they dig in and resist. This is the fast track to becoming dysfunctional. Instead of taking a step back, assessing what needs to change, and adapting to the new situation, traumatized people may double down and put up strong walls of resistance. Instead of feeling excited about learning a new way to do things, they cling to *their* way. Instead of finding ways to leverage their wisdom, or finding new ways to add value, they are unable to pivot or reinvent themselves. Eventually, they can become dysfunctional to the needs of the situation.

They seem angry, aggressive, or "difficult" in other ways. Employees may be disagreeable and contrary (or more so than previously). They may give you unexplained pushback or develop a negative attitude in place of their usual optimism and tenacity. They may have angry outbursts. They may become increasingly unpleasant to work with. Unfortunately, many times this behavior pushes others away when they are most needed for support.

They resort to self-destructive behaviors to relieve distress. People who have been traumatized may develop an exaggerated stress response. This occurs when the stress they're feeling crosses over into *distress*. In the face of stress people can still (with difficulty) get back on track moving toward their goals. With distress the new and highest priority goal becomes finding a way to relieve it. People may resort to excess drinking, eating, avoidance behaviors, overworking, etc., to numb or mask their pain. These behaviors can be counterproductive methods to cope and can be a slippery slope if they become habits or addictions.

They insist they are "fine" or go uncharacteristically silent. Trauma-induced behaviors don't always show up as negatives. Yet when people refuse to acknowledge they are impacted at all, especially when others are clearly struggling, it's often a sign that they're masking their pain. An interesting observation about people is that when you ask them how they're doing and they reply, "Great," they're usually good. However, when they reply, "Fine," they very well might not be.

Leaders behave in un-leaderly ways. Remember, these red flags signifying trauma don't just appear in employees. Leaders are just as susceptible to traumatic impact as employees. For example, a leader might seem paralyzed and abdicate responsibility—hiding out in their office and not doing what they need to do to lead the company out of trouble. On the other hand, they might overreact and make rash, knee-jerk decisions even though they were previously known for levelheaded steadiness.

WHY IT'S SO IMPORTANT TO RECOGNIZE THE SIGNS & SYMPTOMS OF TRAUMA

Now you know some of the main ways that trauma shows up in individuals in the workplace. Be on the lookout for them. Recognizing these signs and symptoms is the first step in guiding employees and your fellow leaders through crises of all kinds and ultimately help the organization heal. Here are a few reasons it is important to be able to recognize the signs and symptoms of trauma.

It signals that someone needs help. Anyone struggling with trauma needs and deserves support and understanding. As a leader it is your responsibility to intervene and get them the help they need. (See tips below for how you can deal effectively with your own traumatic stress.)

It helps you realize people are not resisting change or resisting you. Instead you understand that they're holding onto ways of doing things that no longer work as an act of self-preservation. You will realize they're not trying to be difficult. Rather, they are acting out of fear and uncertainty. When you know people are doing the best they can in bad circumstances, that can quickly defuse your feeling negatively toward them.

. . . which keeps you from judging or punishing them. Without recognizing trauma for what it is, you may write off unsavory behavior as "Sam's just crazy" or "Bob has lost his mind." Or worse, you may let go a perfectly good employee who simply needs a little support and understanding.

. . . which allows you to respond in a way that helps employees heal rather than escalating conflicts. Calling out or scolding an employee for normal trauma responses only leads to further resistance and escalation (perhaps on both your parts). Recognizing trauma for what it is helps you circumnavigate this trap and get on a better path, quicker.

. . . which, in turn strengthens your relationship. All of this can rapidly deescalate conflicts between you and them. Furthermore, when they feel more understood than criticized, they have less need to be self-protective, guarded toward you, and reactive against you. When their defensiveness turns to appreciation for your understanding and compassion, that can make them want to cooperate with you instead of pushing back.

It helps you recognize trauma in yourself. For example, maybe you are lashing out at a colleague. Or maybe you have the urge to retreat to your office and hide. When you know why you are feeling the way you are, you can take a step back, assess, and shift your behavior to a more appropriate one.

It enables you to teach others why they feel the way they feel. Once people become aware of how they show up when they are afraid or insecure, they can start facing and changing undesired behaviors.

Ultimately, you are able to get the focus off of people's "bad behavior." This frees you up to start making healthy and productive changes that make life better for everyone. It is amazing how much leaders can accomplish when they are not constantly having to address "problem" employees.

Most importantly, recognizing trauma helps you intervene in time to stop tensions before they boil over. We already know panic is contagious. The sooner you recognize and address trauma, the sooner you can nip the "panic bug" in the bud . . . and the better off everyone will be.

This is especially vital in crises that are ongoing, like our current situation with COVID-19. Individuals in your organization may face long-term uncertainty, continued risk of illness, possible layoffs or furloughs, and physical separation for perhaps the next year or even longer. When leaders are prepared to identify trauma in individuals, you can intercede and get people the support they need. This helps them now *and* sets them up to navigate the crises that will inevitably follow this one.

Finally, never forget that that you too are an *individual* worthy of healing and support. At the same time, you are responsible for leading an organization—come what may. While it is no easy task to lead through trauma, especially while being impacted yourself, it is possible. In fact, it can be a growth experience.

DEALING WITH TRAUMATIC STRESS: PROFESSIONAL HELP AND SELF-CARE

Do you or your employees need professional help to deal with the impacts of traumatic stress? It depends. Not everyone requires treatment. Most people recover on their own with time. But when distress is interfering with normal function or relationships, that's a red flag that someone may need psychological help. Therapeutic interventions like Psychological First Aid (initially created to help people cope in the aftermath of terrorism or some other disaster) or Cognitive Behavioral Therapy (which teaches people how to change harmful thought and behavior patterns) can be incredibly helpful.

In many cases, self-care can go a long way toward speeding the healing process. You have no doubt heard the airplane safety instructions about putting your own oxygen mask on before you can help others. This is true for leaders but it is just as true for employees. Everyone needs to practice self-care—especially in times of traumatic stress.

At first glance practices like getting enough sleep, eating well, exercising, and talking to loved ones may seem overly simple or self-evident. However, they're more important than most of us realize in keeping us mentally, emotionally, and of course physically healthy.

In times of "normal" stress we might neglect one or two self-care practices. For example, we stay up too late, skip meals (or wolf down fast food at our desk), or skip our normal workout routine. While it's not ideal, it's typically not extremely harmful. But when short-term stress moves to long-term trauma the effects go on and on . . . and that's when we get into trouble.

A few nights of burning the midnight oil may not be a big deal. Week after week of missed sleep is. And that's just one area of neglect. If you're missing out on three or four or more parts of your normal self-care routine, things can quickly snowball.

All that said, we recommend that you share this Self-Care Checklist with your employees as a "gentle reminder" during times of stress and/or trauma.

SELF-CARE CHECKLIST

- ❑ Getting enough sleep? (Most adults need 7 to 9 hours a night to function at their best.)
- ❑ Eating a healthy, well-balanced diet?
- ❑ Getting regular exercise? (Ideally, you need 150 minutes of moderate exercise like walking each week, or 75 minutes of more intense activity.)
- ❑ Taking breaks when you feel stressed out?
- ❑ Avoiding drugs and alcohol?
- ❑ Seeking out healthy coping strategies like massage, meditation, spending time in nature, etc.?

❑ Spending enough time with friends and family members? (Talking to loved ones about your experiences and feelings can be extremely helpful.)

❑ Asking others to relieve your burden where they can? (This can mean asking family members to take over household chores that you normally do in order to give you a much-needed break.)

❑ Seeking the support of a counselor, doctor, or clergyperson?

❑ Spending time socializing with friends and/or pursuing fun activities with family members?

❑ Staying engaged and active in life outside of work? (This could be anything from volunteering to helping a neighbor to learning a new hobby—anything that takes your mind off the trauma and the stress you are under.)

Finally, urge employees to be patient. It takes time to recover from a traumatic event. Tell them to be as kind to themselves as possible and try to adhere to their normal routine as much as they can. Keep in mind the saying "this too shall pass." One day they—and you—will realize that the trauma has passed and life is moving on.

Sometimes when the trauma seems to forever change the world, you may discover that moving through it and past it is just a matter of *learning to live with life never being the same again.* That doesn't mean it's over, nor does it mean that you can never be happy.

Leaders, we hope that you will apply what you are learning in this book to help yourself heal from trauma. It's the best gift you can give yourself and your organization as you work to make it stronger and more successful.

CHAPTER 4

HOW TRAUMA DISRUPTS YOUR ORGANIZATION

WHEN DIANA FIRST began talking with leaders and groups about organizational trauma following her experience leading through a horrific workplace shooting, her message was met with interest but also with some head scratching. Surely *individuals* are traumatized when disaster strikes, but how is the organization *itself* traumatized? Exploring that question is the crux of this chapter.

While it's rarely talked about in these terms (though, hopefully, that is changing), crises *can* and *do* impact organizations in a way that moves them beyond stress and into the realm of trauma. The more Diana's story was shared—and the more common threads we found linking that horrific hospital shooting to their own, seemingly less-dire events—the clearer it became that many organizations were showing the trauma response.

And of course we can't forget the collective trauma that 2020 has been. The events of last year have brought the phenomenon home to many of us in a very personal way. When COVID-19 hit, within days workplaces shut down and people transitioned to home offices. Few businesses had plans in place for dealing with a pandemic, and it showed. The ability to conduct normal operations was disrupted in the short-term, and in many cases companies are still severely compromised.

The COVID-19 crisis underscores the need to learn how to deal with organizational trauma *now*. We need to take this as an opportunity to get familiar with the characteristics and the patterns that emerge inside organizations in the wake of a traumatic event.

Remember, trauma can show up in the form of a single dramatic event (like an act of violence, a natural disaster, or the death of a beloved coworker) or it can be ongoing or cumulative (like sexual harassment, systemic racism, discrimination, the ongoing threat of layoffs, etc.). Either way, trauma disrupts, debilitates, and damages the organization either temporarily or long-term. It compromises your workforce, your structures, and your systems.

The faster we recognize trauma as trauma, the faster we can heal from it. This doesn't just mean intervening with individuals but also with entire organizations. And it isn't only about putting the pieces back after a crisis has happened. It's also about putting solid tools, processes, and systems in place so that we are well-prepared for future crises. We all need a roadmap going forward.

Before we continue, one caveat: We use the broad word "organization" in this book, but we really mean *any* collection or group of people organized for a common purpose. These ideas may work for businesses, community groups, nonprofits, education systems, and so forth. Our roadmap is designed for all.

INITIAL REACTIONS PREDICT LONG-TERM OUTCOMES

Now let's take a look at what happens in an organization in the aftermath of a traumatic event. As soon as a trauma occurs the organization's immediate priorities center around survival. This usually consists of ensuring immediate safety and security, assessing the current situation, containment (if possible), communicating and reporting the situation, and assessing potential for additional risk moving forward.

When organizations do these things effectively in the short-term it bodes well for their long-term success. However, most typically *do not* do these things well (or at least they don't do *all* of them well). Ineffective actions taken can further damage the culture of the organization.

Here's the scary truth: Most organizations are simply not prepared to respond to a traumatic crisis. Leaders are left to make it up as they go.

This lack of preparation is a serious problem for most organizations. Very few of them (outside of healthcare and law enforcement) have well-developed "Incident Command"-like processes and structures in place to rapidly respond to a crisis. Few leaders have had much practice in real life-threatening situations or drills. These skills are simply not in their wheelhouse.

What's more, there is rarely a clearly defined structure in place for making quick decisions. There is often a lack of clarity around duties and responsibilities. There is no plan for communicating quickly and clearly. There is no method for obtaining and centrally processing information and facts. All of this leaves organizations vulnerable.

Sure, most companies will do a fire drill from time to time, but most people don't take them very seriously. There's little attention paid to such exercises, and even less paid to disaster preparedness in general.

Few companies even have backup plans in place for acquiring *essentials* in the event of a trauma or crisis. There are no guidelines for keeping the supply chain intact. There's no plan for what to do in the case of a telecom or utility outage.

Unfortunately, there is a huge downside to avoiding these preparations: When a disaster occurs, people are forced to make it up as they go. This seldom ends well.

IT'S NOT ALL BAD NEWS

There is a bright spot in any crisis and it's this: When trauma first strikes, people can and do rise to the occasion. There's an immediate sense of camaraderie. This is when you see altruism and acts of great heroism as people come to the rescue of others. People often behave more kindly and generously to one another and experience the best in others, even in cultures where negativity and toxicity also exist. It's a paradox: In the worst of times we often get to witness the best of humanity.

As we discussed in chapter 3, surviving a trauma can even be a bonding experience. (Remember, this is the result of the so-called fourth F, *friend*.) Experiencing an event together deepens our connections with each other. If leaders knew how to intentionally leverage this sense of camaraderie and use it to unify the organization, that would be great. Unfortunately, this rarely happens.

What does frequently happen is that individuals bond with like-minded coworkers and end up splitting into factions. People begin to question other peoples' motives and start taking sides. This division can deepen into outright polarization. (We'll explain how this sequence unfolds in the next section.)

We can look to COVID-19 for an example of this splintering on a national level. Think back to the start of the pandemic. Initially, we were all "in it together." But then as the impacts of COVID-19 became more apparent—and in the absence of a clear and unifying approach for handling the virus—cracks appeared in our unity. They deepened into chasms. People began voicing opinions about who was to blame and what was to be done until the topic became deeply polarizing. (See chapter 5 for a deeper exploration of this subject.)

HOW LACK OF PREPAREDNESS
AND STRUCTURE IMPACTS ORGANIZATIONS

When you aren't prepared and a trauma occurs, predictably, a chain reaction of negative consequences unfolds. Here is a typical sequence of outcomes. Things may not happen precisely this way (all organizations are different and so are the crises they face) but you can expect the future to unfold something like this:

- **The lack of a plan exacerbates the fear people are feeling.** When a crisis happens, people experience the fight/flight/freeze survival response that we discussed in chapter 3. Uncertainty runs rampant. Employees panic. Of course, having a plan in place would counteract (or at least mitigate) all that. When employees know you're not just making knee-jerk decisions, they feel safer and remain calm. Without a plan the chaos multiplies, feeding the fear and making everything worse.

- **There's no clarity around roles and this creates confusion.** People will ask *"Who is in charge?"* Often the answer is not immediately clear, especially when multiple agencies and divisions are involved, or when an event occurs after business hours and the leadership team is not onsite. There is no clarity around duties and responsibilities. Then the question becomes, *"If we can't get ahold of the leader, who's in charge?"* People often end up on a long phone tree trying to figure out who needs to be involved. None of this is very coordinated because there isn't an established process to follow. And even when people do know who is in charge, it's often not clear how things are being handled, or how decisions are being made. This lack of clarity increases anxiety because those decisions impact every individual.

- **Having no "common language" to convey that a trauma has occurred makes it difficult to activate people and teams.** Diana shares that in the hospitals, the nomenclature for a disaster was "Code Triage." Everybody knew what that meant, knew their role, and knew where they were supposed to go and what they were supposed to do. However most businesses don't have that mechanism. Without the common language it's difficult to alert people when a crisis occurs, assign roles, activate teams, and create a needed sense of urgency.

- **Leader behavior can be inconsistent, worsening the situation.** Remember, leaders are traumatized as well when something goes badly for an organization. Different leaders have different responses to traumatic stress. Some may move into "command and control" mode while others may disappear and seem to abdicate their responsibility. Besides hampering the likelihood that employees will do what they need to do, inconsistent leader behavior makes people feel even more panicked.

- **Absence of a formal system for collecting and centralizing information hampers sound decision-making.** When a crisis occurs, it can be difficult to collect information about what has happened, what damage has been done, who has been affected, what additional risks still exist, and so forth. Plus, misinformation and rumors make it difficult to sort through what is accurate and what is not. Sometimes a trauma is over within minutes, but many times it's still unfolding. Without a well-developed system for gathering information, obtaining updates, and processing and analyzing data, an organization is further thrown into chaos and confusion.

- **Lack of clarity around how decisions will be made ramps up chaos.** It's hard to solve problems rationally and make quick, sound decisions in a chaotic environment. This in turn adds to the confusion, increases fear, and reinforces the appearance that the organization is disorganized.

- **Communication falters and stokes fear, confusion, and possibly anger.** In the immediate wake of crisis or shortly thereafter, communication is often lacking or inadequate. Perhaps this is because the leaders say "I don't have all the information so we'll communicate when we do," or "We'll tell them when they need to know." But, if there is a process for saying "We see you. We hear you. We will get you information ASAP," people will feel confident that the situation is being handled and contained.

- **Leader communication that is "too little too late" creates distrust, lack of confidence, and insecurity.** Often a leader will put out one memo and think to themselves, "I told everybody . . . I did my part." In the leader's defense, they *did* do what they were supposed to do. The leader may even get defensive, saying. "I did tell! People just aren't reading their emails!" But it's not a matter of whether you are writing the memo or not; one mode of communication alone may be ineffective. If people aren't reading your emails you need to find other modalities because you need the end result to be that people are informed. We will cover several tactics for better communication in chapter 7.

- **Narratives that arise to fill the voids are usually negative.** In the absence of clear communication, a void opens up. And unfortunately, people don't generally fill voids with positive narratives, especially when they are in survival mode. Instead, they go into guessing mode and jump to conclusions, which many times can veer far from the truth. This is not malice. It's just that when people need answers and don't get them, they are likely to assume the worst.

It's also worth noting that in a communication void, leaders also make things up. They create narratives about what they think people know. But often they are wrong in these assumptions, and employees may be aware of much less than leaders assume they know.

When a trauma suddenly hits and leaders don't see a clear way through it, that can cause them to feel incompetent, lose confidence and feel out of control. This can cause them to feel "out of sorts," meaning they can't sort their way through the trauma, and that can lead to fear-based narratives that are often counterproductive.

- **A wide range of points of view, reference points, perspectives, and conflicting opinions make themselves known.** All, or many, in the organization experience the trauma but not all experience trauma in exactly the same way. Much like how the COVID-19 pandemic has produced a wide range of symptoms (physically and financially), from mild to lethal, a person's unique point of view, access to information, and direct involvement or impact influences how they think, feel, and respond to trauma.

- **Why? becomes the big question.** Blame and guilt (and often shame) creep in. Though it shows up in varying degrees, blame, guilt, and shame are common patterns that linger in organizations that have been traumatized. Here's how they manifest:

First comes *blame.* Once news of the trauma becomes known, *why* becomes the most important question. In that quest to get answers, a whole series of accusations unfold: *Someone should have prevented that! Someone should have known! Why didn't the organization protect us? Who caused this to happen?* The transition from *what* to *why* happens very quickly, and often there's a lot of blame in the subtext of the question, "Why?" Eventually people start to ask "who is to blame?" And, "Who is responsible for what has happened?"

Depending on the kind of trauma that has taken place, guilt can set in as well. People may think things like, "I should have known my coworker was on the brink, was suicidal," or "I saw a sign that something was wrong with the financials, but I didn't take it seriously enough" or "I can't believe I missed that clue," or "I should have been able to save that patient."

Where there is moral injury, there can also be deep shame. Usually moral injury occurs when a trauma is human-caused, when there's a belief that a human decision caused the trauma to occur, or when someone was directed to do something that then led to injury or the death of other humans. People grappling with shame may wonder, "How could that happen here?" or "What kind of organization allows this to happen?" or "What does this say about us and our values?"

One example of such shame might spring from the discovery of ongoing sexual harassment or assault by one member of the organization toward another. People might feel shame that they have a coworker who would do such a thing, shame that there isn't a process for preventing it, and/or shame that people perhaps looked the other way and allowed it to happen.

- **Polarization or division commonly emerges and deepens if it is not effectively addressed.** Blame combined with opinions about why the trauma happened, can create an *us and them* mentality. It becomes even harder to avoid when a trauma happens from within or stems from someone who is not an outsider, or a common enemy. But even in the case of an *external* event like the COVID-19 pandemic, the rise of factions can lead to second-guessing about what's to be done going forward. If there's not much communication about how or why things are being done (remember, lack of communication creates voids), if decision-making is not clear, or if conflict-management skills are not strong or demonstrated by leadership, we see the cracks deepen.

And regardless of what side people are on, an ineffective organizational response can sow further distrust and insecurity and fail to restore a sense of physical and psychological safety. Extreme polarization and division often occurs in organizations that have not been transparent, trustworthy, or reliable. This is especially likely to happen if the organization is secretive, not forthcoming, and has not fostered a strong sense of belonging prior to the trauma. In the next chapter, we will talk about how polarization—and the false choices that can surface as a result of division—can damage an organization, and how *both/and* thinking is key to solving many of an organization's problems both after a trauma occurs and thereafter.

- **Ultimately, all of these factors destroy an organization's culture, its brand, and its reputation.** When people are not kept well informed in the aftermath of a trauma, many derogatory and accusatory things may be said about the organization. This can stir up a lot of negativity, which impacts trust and respect in the organization. People feel unsafe. There is decreased engagement and a rise in cynicism. Long-cherished beliefs about the culture are shattered.

When trauma disrupts a mission-driven organization, values are often challenged. Many organizations have a posted list of values (e.g., treating others with respect, inclusivity, speaking up without fear of reprisal, teamwork and collaboration), but when people are stressed and traumatized, weaknesses in their consistent and widespread adoption are often exposed. Eventually, these values erode, creating lasting negative effects. At that point, the organization itself may ask "Can we be trusted by the community?" Employees may look at one another and ask, "Can we trust each other?" and "Can we trust the organization to keep us safe?"

Of course trauma will not just expose hypocrisy around values. It also exposes cracks and weaknesses around operations (issues with communication, decision-making, conflict management), performance (devastating financial impacts), and turnover. Organizations lose good people and then they have trouble recruiting new ones. Existing leaders and employees may wonder, "What's our story?" Meanwhile new people coming in ask "What happened here?"

All of these factors underscore the need to have a plan in place *before* a crisis occurs. Once it happens emotions will run rampant, and the more uncertainty there is, the more emotional things will get. A plan made up of strong processes and systems will allow you to respond rather than react. You can do this by establishing a Rapid Response Process that enables fast, sound decision-making. We will learn more about it in chapter 6.

When a trauma occurs, *everyone* needs to know their role, their responsibilities and specifically what they are accountable for and to whom, so that others can count on them. Leaders must be able to show up in a calm and contained way. Employees need a role to play, too. Giving them a checklist of tasks creates structure and a sense of security. As a leader you may be incident commander but it's not a dictatorship. Other people can pull you aside and advise you so you can take various viewpoints into consideration.

A strong plan also requires that you have a solid system in place for communication. Everyone needs to be well-informed so there are no assumptions and guesswork. Again, we will learn more about leader communication tactics in chapter 7.

Above all, we are all in this together. When crisis strikes we need to know how to leverage the fourth F, *friend*. We can call out acts of heroism and do-gooding to reinforce this natural camaraderie that occurs alongside the worst disasters. Remember, if we don't intentionally unify, the culture can easily, and too often does, turn negative and lead to the sharp divisions and polarization you will learn about in the next chapter.

CHAPTER 5

DEALING WITH POLARIZATION AND THE BAD DECISIONS IT CREATES

IT'S NATURAL FOR opposing views to exist within organizations. The debates around them are often healthy and helpful. But as we discussed in the last chapter, when traumatic events occur this natural phenomenon can be taken to the extreme. Strongly held contrasting points of view emerge—why something happened, who is at fault, and what's to be done—and people split into factions around those points of view.

Very quickly, the rifts deepen. People become entrenched on one side or the other, with each side believing that it's right and the other is decidedly wrong. These beliefs are rigid and resistant to change. Debates become heated (or, as is often the case, people silently seethe) and people become further pitted against one another.

The upshot is that the organization gets trapped in an either/or mindset. People become convinced (mistakenly) that a choice must be made between one side or the other. That's polarization. Even in the best circumstances buying into such a false choice is extremely damaging to an organization's culture. But in the throes of trauma, it can be toxic and have destructive, even lethal consequences. As you will learn, it sets off a pendulum swing that sends the organization careening from one deeply flawed "solution" to another.

Before we talk about how polarization manifests inside organizations, let's look at the phenomenon in a different context. Polarization also harms societies and nations. Let's take a look at a case study that Americans are painfully familiar with these days.

THE FALSE CHOICE OF COVID-19: A HEALTHY ECONOMY OR A HEALTHY POPULACE

When the COVID-19 pandemic kicked off in early 2020, widespread fear of the virus and its potential to catastrophically wipe us out forced our nation to make a quick decision. Our leaders determined that we needed to do everything possible to ensure our physical survival in the short run. In retrospect this was completely understandable, expected, and necessary. In the face of a frightening new virus we couldn't afford to *not* react swiftly and definitively.

At first, an overall feeling of "we're all in this together" predominated. En masse we moved into survival mode. We hunkered down, sheltered in place at home, and closed businesses and schools. There were a few dissenting voices but for the most part we were willing to ensure the health of the populace at any cost. We bonded together around that goal.

Alongside the fear and chaos of those early weeks was a palpable "can-do" attitude. A spirit of innovation appeared as we scrambled to work from home and transition our children to virtual education. Oh sure, tempers flared and nerves frayed at the suddenness and the complication of converting our lives overnight, but we also saw altruism. Neighbors reached out to help neighbors. Citizens did their best to support local businesses impacted by the shutdown. Entire cities joined forces to cheer on their healthcare heroes.

In other words, people pretty readily adapted to the shutdown. They stayed home in order to ensure that people didn't get the virus or infect someone else. And though they were shaken and worried they stayed unified and vigilant . . . for a little while.

CRACKS APPEAR IN THE UNITY

The upside of reacting swiftly and shutting down was that it gave us time to learn more about how the virus was transmitted and get a handle on the outbreak. And, outside of the early hot spots, most regions were not overwhelmed with hospitalizations. Though infections and deaths continued to increase, most people were not directly impacted by death or illness, nor even knew anyone who had gotten it.

After a month of shutdowns and staying at home, there were signs that the curve was beginning to flatten. That was good news, but it also signaled the start of serious division in the ranks. For many, it seemed the danger had passed or wasn't as catastrophic (at least for them) as they had originally thought it might be. People questioned whether the numbers of illnesses or deaths were even real, or if they'd been inflated.

And though we'd begun to reap some of the upsides of focusing on health, we also began to feel the downsides of our willingness to go "all out" to fight the virus, of initially choosing the health of the populace at any cost. The shutdown created furloughs, then outright job losses, and many business closures. The financial impact was felt by almost everyone. Unemployment rates skyrocketed. For most businesses, revenue cratered.

While a little had been done to try to bridge these losses from the shutdown (most notably the CARES Act which was signed into law in late March), we couldn't keep up with the enormity and reach of the impact. The government was unwilling or unable to pursue more financial safety net measures. And as the shutdown dragged on many people faced financial devastation . . . and most others experienced intense anxiety, insecurity, and outright fear of financial catastrophe.

Plus, there were other downsides. People had grown weary of actions taken to curb the spread of the virus. They missed "normal" life, missed seeing loved ones, missed going out.

It soon became clear that factions were emerging. The choice between continuing the shutdown to ensure the health of the populace or reopening to restore a healthy economy became a flashpoint. It created division and pitted people against one another. It didn't help that the factions followed along political party lines.

Ideally, a wise leader would have pointed out that we were grappling with a false choice. We didn't have to choose one over the other. We could find solutions that achieved both desired outcomes: a healthy populace and a healthy economy. But that didn't happen. So the rift deepened. And was strengthened because we did not lead from the beginning with the idea of unity as a nation or even unity globally.

THE PENDULUM SWINGS

With increasing, frantic concerns over economic survival, the pendulum began to swing toward the other side—toward reopening—*even if it meant increased infection rates or deaths.*

As states began to reopen, many tried to not choose economic health solely over public health. Instead they instituted a hybrid, step-wise approach to reopening. But there was little coordination or agreement on a systematic national game plan. The reopenings were haphazard, communication was inconsistent, and we saw limited adherence to guidelines. Even the simple act of wearing a mask to protect oneself and others became entrenched in political polarization.

Of course, viruses don't honor state lines. Soon the downsides of overfocusing on the health of the economy by haphazardly reopening became apparent when we experienced a second surge in infections and deaths—even larger than the previous one.

To add insult to injury, the great reopening wasn't, financially, as great as hoped. People were reluctant to come back out in full force the way business owners and some government officials thought they would. This made the economic recovery anemic. Unfortunately, people came back out just enough (mostly in social settings like parties, rallies, and the Sturgis Motorcycle Rally) to result in a third, even bigger, spike in infections but not a rebound of the economy.

Not surprisingly the pendulum is now swinging toward another shutdown, at least in some locations.

A GRIM FUTURE

Any new shutdown will likely once again curb infection and death rates and lead to a new plateau. But at the same time, it will almost certainly result in even more financial hardship and economic ruin on top of a slow rebound. Then most likely we can expect another swing of the pendulum. This is how the pattern plays out.

Without remaining united—and without noticing the choice between the economy and health is largely a false one—we may have quickly become stuck in intractable polarization that has disastrous consequences with each swing of the pendulum. With each vacillation between one extreme and the other we can expect more wasted resources, time, energy, money . . . and lost lives.

In other words, if we don't arrest the pendulum swing, we could be in even deeper trouble. There are many examples of polarization in our society, but few are as intertwined and connected to our survival and long-term thriving as the economy and public health. With deepening polarization, rigid, intractable either/or mentality, fatigue, anger, and blame, we're close to an outright stalemate. We're headed toward the worst-case scenario of ending up on the downsides of both "solutions" which would be catastrophic: lots of death *and* a collapsed economy.

As you can hopefully see by now, when we resort to either/or thinking, at best we end up with winners and losers (and eventually everyone loses). But it doesn't have to be that way.

A BETTER WAY

Ask yourself this: *What if we had it to do over again? What if we had not fallen into the trap believing we had a false choice to make? What if, instead of believing we had to choose between ensuring the health of as many people as possible or safeguarding the economy we had chosen instead to focus on a higher goal? What if we had aimed for coming up with solutions that optimized both sides?*

What if we'd identified "health vs. economy" as a false choice, spoken about it in those terms, talked about the consequences of focusing on one to the detriment of the other, and communicated a clear plan that showed how both were possible, that made choosing both compelling?

Chances are, everything would be different right now.

Because of the scale and size of the COVID-19 pandemic, this is a chance to shift our mindset from the either/or paradigm to one that encompasses both/and. We've long been trapped in the false choice of economy vs. public health in terms of government spending. Even in normal situations, we can't realistically have a healthy economy without healthy people and vice versa. When one side is favored the downsides eventually emerge.

But here's the difference: Typically the pendulum swing to the other side occurs over years (usually with changing administrations or congressional majorities) and is not as readily apparent. Until the pandemic, the stakes were not widespread, high, and catastrophic enough to get our collective attention.

Now, we have the opportunity to arrest the pendulum. It's not too late! We could leverage the positives of both sides to create something better than what existed before. We could create policies and processes that result in a stronger economy *and* a healthier populace in the long run and mitigate the devastating damage we've experienced thus far.

Now, let's move back to the organizational realm. Similar polarizations occur inside companies. The key is to operationalize "Polarity Thinking." When we do, we'll be able to reject the "false choice" paradigm and create solutions to leverage both sides rather than choosing one over the other. In this way we can transform an organization. Making this shift is a game changer.

POLARITY THINKING IS THE SOLUTION

First things first: "Polarities" are interdependent pairs of conditions, values, characteristics, preferences, and attributes that seemingly represent opposing sides, and present as tensions, choices, or either/or dilemmas. They are the "sides" we've been talking about and they exist at the organization level and the individual level. Upon examination, they are false choices.

"Polarity Thinking" is a term coined by Barry Johnson (founder of Polarity Partnerships) in the 1990s. It reflects the model he developed to describe polarization at the organizational and individual level, and methods for managing them. (See www.polaritypartnerships.com.)

Over the years, Barry and his colleagues (and many others who study polarities within organizations) have identified many examples of commonly occurring polarities at an organizational level. Here are several examples, framed as either/or questions:

COMMON POLARITIES AT THE ORGANIZATIONAL LEVEL

- Mission or margin?
- High quality or low cost?
- Speedy decisions or involved decisions?
- Continuity/consistency in services or innovative/transformational offerings?
- Short-term achievement or success in the long run?
- Financial performance or employee engagement?
- Individual autonomy or accountability to the whole?
- Individual excellence or exceptional teamwork?
- Depth of expertise or synergy across business units?
- Centralized functions or decentralized operations?

When asked to choose between these polarities, theoretically most of us would reject the false choice and say we want both. But tugs-of-war between them often play out under our conscious radar (even though the effects of choosing one side over the other, the "downsides," are often clearly evident in the organization).

In practice, when our processes, policies, and behaviors are overly focused on one side but neglect the other, there are consequences as the downsides begin to emerge. But these downsides usually present as a "problem to solve" rather than a polarity to manage, and the solutions to it usually result in a swing in the pendulum to the other, previously unchosen side. Eventually, the downsides or "problems" of over-focusing on the other side emerge and the pendulum swings yet again.

Typically, preferences for one side are deeply rooted in the organization's values and beliefs. And since the pendulum swing cycle is often very long—years in many cases—they are not easily observable or identifiable. In other words, the organization compensates for, rather than addressing and managing, these polarities.

And while these polarities may remain under the conscious radar during normal, business-as-usual times, a traumatic event can stoke and inflame polarization. This can reveal how detrimental (and outright damaging in some cases) polarities are when the stakes are high and they are not effectively identified and addressed.

Take decision-making. This is often framed as a choice between having processes or a leadership style that enables a business to *either* make quick decisions (flat organization structure, single authority, command and control style) *or* get a lot of input and involvement (committees, layers, formal approval processes, consensus style). But in a crisis, organizations need both. It must *both* be clear who is in charge and how decisions are to be made *and* there must be a way to ensure adequate input and involvement by many. This is not business as usual; it's new and unfamiliar territory. Without a both/and approach chaos and confusion are certain to ensue.

Organizations function well when we can reject either/or thinking and leverage both sides of these polarity pairs with a "both/and" approach. While we can acknowledge that polarities will always exist in our organizations, we can learn to leverage them. We can intentionally design structures and create a leadership mindset to maximize the effects of both sides and minimize the downsides of each—and achieve things we couldn't otherwise.

As mentioned, polarities show up at the individual level as well. We often have a preference, comfort level, or strong beliefs about which one is right or stronger—which one we value. And a search of the literature shows the "experts" have these preferences too. Quite often, the advice from one source contradicts the advice from another. For example, one source may advise "Be in command, take charge, be proactive, take the initiative" while another recommends "Get everyone on board, make sure all are included." Taking it all in is sure to give a leader whiplash!

Approached with an either/or mindset, choosing one or the other will more likely result in a short-term gain, but at the expense of long-term outcomes. Or it may set the organization up for success in the future but greatly imperil it in the short run. The wise approach is to frame it as a "both/and" and to develop a skillset to know when to use one and also how to leverage both.

INDIVIDUAL LEADER POLARITIES

In a crisis and in everyday situations an effective leader *both* . . .

- Takes charge *and* builds consensus [everyone knows who is in charge and many are involved].
- Displays calm, steady demeanor *and* demonstrates vulnerability [models equanimity and is human, genuine, real].
- Demonstrates resolve and commitment to goals *and* is adaptable and flexible as new information arises and new developments emerge [is firm and convicted but not stubborn, is flexible but not wishy-washy].
- Develops and implements strategies for the short-term *and* the long run.
- Can zero in on details *and* see the big picture [sees trees and forest].
- Effectively advocates for their own ideas, solutions, and beliefs *and* remains open to and curious about others' ideas.
- Focuses on getting results *and* on building healthy relationships.
- Inspires people around the collective purpose and vision of the organization *and* is tactical and action-oriented [talks and walks].
- Is direct and candid *and* diplomatic and tactful.

- Demonstrates confidence *and* humility [knows what they know and what they don't, doesn't MSU (make sh*t up) to cover for lack of knowledge, acknowledges others have answers/information/knowledge].

Evaluate yourself in each of these pairs. Which pairs resonate most with you? Do you see yourself picking one side, having a preference for one side over the other? Does your preference change when you're under stress? Identify the costs of remaining entrenched in one side and neglecting developing the other. Consider seeking feedback from others—ask if they see you as strongly demonstrating one side but not the other.

As with the organizational level, both sides in these polarities are needed. In different circumstances leaders must leverage seemingly contrasting and opposite skills, mindsets, and strengths. Understanding these polarities and being able to move between them as needed is important for any leader who must navigate their organization through trauma. This showcases just how hard it is to be a great leader—and underscores the need for good leader training inside an organization.

WHAT HAPPENS WHEN POLARIZATION GOES UNCHECKED?

So what's at stake when polarities aren't well managed—particularly in a deeply divided, emotionally charged environment following a trauma when either/or thinking can be catastrophic? Here's an example of the fallout you can expect:

- Obviously, you don't get a workable solution. The best solution pulls from both sides.
- There is damage to your culture, brand, etc. The pitting of individuals against each other often leads to people fleeing or being jettisoned.

- This in turn harms morale, trust, belonging, engagement, and causes eventual floundering of company. There may be lost productivity, lost market share, eroded public trust and reputation.
- Just as today's problems were yesterday's solutions, today's solutions become tomorrow's problems. All of this back and forth damages leader credibility with employees. They say "here we go again." They don't take things seriously after a while.
- On a small scale, the impact of trauma may be contained and not have a major impact in the community. A company might go out of business or be reinvested. People usually are then able to find new jobs. However, when you apply either/or to a larger industry there can be a lot more damage (think auto manufacturing or coal mining, both of which took communities down with them). And when a nation is polarized and trapped in either/or thinking the damage is enormous (as we've all now witnessed or directly experienced during the COVID-19 pandemic).

When an organization has been traumatized it's imperative to address any polarization that arises so that you don't fall into false choices that emerge. You can expect issues to flare up and deepen. And you can expect to be initially conflicted by choices pitting short-term survival with success in the long run.

Logically, if you can't survive today, you won't be around tomorrow. But when the decision does not take the long view into consideration, that future is damaged. For example, when a business faces significant financial challenges, it will often choose to make decisions to shore up its financial health at the expense of employee engagement. It's not that taking action to ensure financial health is wrong—it's that employee engagement must also be considered and addressed and not neglected when those actions are being decided.

BREAKING THE POLARIZATION CYCLE (YES, WE CAN!)

So now that you see what polarities are and how damaging they can be, how do you defang them? How do you move from either/or thinking to both/and thinking? How do you break free from polarization and get better results and engagement? Is all of this possible? Absolutely! But first you must get real about what you're doing when you decide to break the hold polarization has on your company.

In other words, you have to decide that you really do want to solve these kinds of dilemmas. This is tougher than it sounds. It's easy to continue taking a side, or wrestling for control. Yet this only deepens echo chambers. It's tempting to use "wrong-making" or righteousness as a mechanism for convincing. ("See? We tried it your way and it didn't work.") Ultimately, this just keeps the pendulum swinging back and forth.

To break this cycle leaders need to stop proposing solutions before getting clear about the goals to be achieved. Let's say you are trying to decide between, say, centralization and decentralization. One way is to reframe the goal, not as a choice between centralization or decentralization, but, rather, the goal is stated at a higher level, for example: to establish processes and systems that capture the benefits of both and minimize the downsides of each. Thus, you'd frame it as a "both/and" situation.

You'd start by identifying all the upsides of decentralization (innovativeness, autonomy, and speed to name a few) and then all the benefits of centralization (e.g. efficiency, coordination, synergy). Then you'd identify the downsides that can emerge when a function is purely decentralized (inconsistency, communication breakdowns, lots of duplication) and then identify the downsides of centralization (red tape, bureaucracy, slowness, squelched creativity). You'd discuss how when the downsides show up, they appear as problems—which we often rush to solve by swinging to the other side.

Now, you're in a position to find solutions that will get the upsides of both and develop tactics to minimize or mitigate the downsides of each—rather than simply arguing that one side is best.

Hopefully you are beginning to see that polarity is *not* about compromise or simply balancing between the two. It's not about getting to "50-50" of each side. Sometimes compromise or meeting in the middle is the best first option, but ideally you put processes and solutions in place that leverage both.

It's important to educate people, to show them what the either/or and both/and mindsets look like. Teaching this way of thinking in your organization tends to generate really creative solutions. It gives everyone a common language and invites them to see problems (and state goals) differently.

Also, reward and recognize this behavior when you see it. Make polarity thinking part of your culture.

In a nutshell, polarity thinking empowers us to see another perspective. We learn to see that there are upsides to the opposing viewpoint and that even if we got "our way" there would be downsides to that. By leveraging both polarities we can create something better than we would have had if we settled for one side alone. But, also, we become more flexible, openminded, innovative leaders and employees who are motivated to understand each other even when we don't agree. We become the kind of people the world needs more of.

The tactics we lay out here and in the remaining chapters are, themselves, based on polarity thinking. They are designed to help individuals *and* organizations both heal and recover from trauma *and* grow stronger in the process. They're meant to help you survive in the short-term *and* thrive in the long run. We hope that your journey forward will illustrate the transformative power of polarity thinking in a deeply personal way.

PART 2

A ROADMAP FOR NAVIGATING FUTURE TRAUMAS AND BUSINESS DISRUPTIONS

YOGI BERRA IS FAMOUS FOR SAYING, "IF YOU DON'T KNOW where you're going, you'll end up someplace else." We would add: *And if you don't know how you'll get there, you may not survive the journey.*

Few businesses take time to plan for crisis. This is understandable. It's hard to justify spending resources for unlikely events. Margins and time are so thin that the trade-off is immediate needs, immediate goals. Yet getting intentionally good at crisis planning and putting some best practices in place will make your organization better whether you ever face a major trauma or not.

The clearer you are around what you propose to do in a crisis, why you're doing it, how you'll do it, and what the specific expectations are, the more in control and calmer, safer, more confident, and more hopeful people in the organization will feel—and the less likely you'll make big mistakes that have serious consequences down the road.

As you read this you may at first have trouble relating to the notion that you need a crisis roadmap. After all, dire and terrifying events (fires, earthquakes, workplace shootings) don't happen very often in the grand scheme of things. Thankfully, this is true. These kinds of events are few and far between. But don't stop reading yet.

Before we go any further, consider several points:

- Just because something is unlikely to happen doesn't mean it won't. The COVID-19 pandemic is Exhibit A. Very few people foresaw a pandemic that would require everyone to move their offices home virtually overnight. Yet here we are. Most of us could have used a roadmap to make things go more smoothly.

- Having a process in place also helps with lesser emergencies and other major organizational disruptions. We'll list a few of those in a moment. For now, suffice it to say that the steps can be tailored to fit the scope and scale of your circumstances.

- When you deploy these steps during less dire incidents it sets you up to use them if and when something truly traumatic does happen. And running routine practice drills, in advance, will improve readiness and success during real events.

While we designed this roadmap for trauma, we found having this system in place allows leaders to respond to less traumatic but emergent crises more effectively (the first steps in particular) and that the team-building and decision-making redesign also results in improved performance in routine, everyday work, whether there is a trauma or not. And having a plan in place gives leaders and the employees in their organizations peace of mind that they are prepared for unusual happenings, big or small.

Here are just a few of the business disruptions for which this roadmap could be really helpful:

Wi-Fi/Computer system down
Data hack
Break-in or robbery
Layoffs
Termination of a key employee
Product defect

Restructuring of company

Change of ownership/merger/restructuring

Bringing on outside investors

Death or departure of a senior leader

Serious injury to an employee or customer onsite

Sexual harassment accusation

Embezzlement

Major product changes

Minor fire or flooding

Earthquake (used to be a West Coast problem but spreading)

Electricity loss

Resolution of major vendor relationship

Note that while some of these are catastrophic at various levels, some are lesser but still upsetting snafus. Others aren't even inherently negative but still require a great deal of change or disruption within an organization (we all know even positive change can be stressful). The roadmap is helpful any time you need key leaders across multiple functions to make decisions quickly and have a system to communicate with employees, customers, vendors, media, community, and so forth.

Here is a snapshot of the roadmap we will detail throughout the rest of this book. It's easier to think about it in three phases. Immediate Response Tactics, Stabilizing Tactics, and Organizational Long View Tactics.

PHASE ONE: *Immediate Response Tactics:* What needs to happen when trauma (or a major disruption) has or is occurring?

Create a Rapid Response Process. This includes the following activities:

- Assemble a rapid response team

- Designate the leader in charge
- Select a command center and specify a code word
- Develop the plan for information gathering
- Promote a unifying message
- Implement a communication plan

PHASE TWO: *Stabilizing Tactics:* Once the immediate danger has passed, the trauma is "over" (if a single event) or becomes chronic and ongoing (as with the COVID-19 pandemic) what's needed to stabilize the organization?

- Look back/after action review
- Seek outside help
- Name it . . . unequivocally

PHASE THREE: *Organizational Long View Tactics:* What have we learned and how best to move forward long term?

- Integrate it in meaningful ways
- Evolve team-building philosophy
- Redesign decision-making process

The best practices that make up this road map are informed by experience and bolstered by available research. They are customizable and scalable for any size organization. And they're applicable not just for the organization as a whole, but also for any department, unit, or small team within it.

We hope you will put this roadmap to good use. Not only will it help you weather traumatic crises (and less traumatic ones as well), it will help you become a stronger, more resilient, more unified organization in general.

CHAPTER 6

IMMEDIATE RESPONSE TACTICS

N THIS CHAPTER, we will cover some immediate tactics you can deploy when a trauma or major disruptive event occurs in your organization. Just remember, these same steps work just as well in less traumatic yet still stressful events. Whatever the scope and size of the event, you'll go through the same tactics in triage. These will help you move quickly to navigate change and safeguard your organization.

If you don't have a well-thought-out immediate response plan to follow when a crisis strikes you may create a different set of problems down the road. For example, if you have the wrong leaders in place (or no leaders) you may struggle to calm and unify employees. You may lose valuable time. You may make poor decisions whose negative consequences show up later.

Yet, despite its importance, few companies have a plan for crisis in place at all. And if they do, it's very different from what we're talking about here.

RETHINKING YOUR "EMERGENCY PLAN"

For most businesses, the requirement for an emergency action plan is focused on issues like calling 911, using a fire extinguisher, or evacuating the building. At best an organization may have the occasional fire drill. Even if it has a more advanced "emergency plan"—one that includes, say, role-specific responsibilities and phone trees to account for all employees—it usually isn't well-developed, well-practiced, or well-implemented. It may be buried in a P&P Manual somewhere, and employees and leaders may not be fully trained.

We are *not* slamming this kind of plan. It's very important. (In fact, we recommend you see the OSHA Plan Checklist if you need a good reference.)[1] What we're saying is that, while this is what most people think an emergency plan is, it's really the bare minimum. There is so much more involved in getting a company through a traumatic crisis.

For one thing, the typical emergency plan is focused on a single point in time. Many crises unfold gradually (like COVID-19) and require a different approach.

Without a good plan to lead people through a trauma, crisis, or major disruption there will be chaos and confusion. There will be ambiguity around who is in charge. Leaders will make things up on the fly. Coordination will be haphazard. There will be a flurry of phone calls to ascertain what has happened, to gather information, and to determine a course of action.

Also, it will be difficult to alert employees and communicate what's happening as circumstances change. The lack of information will lead to uncertainty, anxiety, and fear, which in turn may lead to rumors and speculation and allow the seeds of divisiveness and polarization to take root.

The good news is that with a little advance planning you can stop all that. A Rapid Response Process can dramatically change how your company experiences a traumatic crisis.

THE BENEFITS OF A RAPID RESPONSE PROCESS

A Rapid Response Process (also known as an Incident Command System) is a standardized, pre-planned approach for dealing with disruption. Getting one in place helps everyone know exactly what to do so that decisions can be made quickly, efficiently, and with a focus on safety. Here are some of the reasons why it's so beneficial:

- It allows people to move into position quickly so they can spring into action. Delays can be costly.
- It conveys more confidence that the response to a crisis or trauma is organized and not haphazard.
- It allows organizations to control the controllables. Plus, the increase in employee and leader skills and confidence in dealing with crisis or disruptive change, very likely will decrease the number of things that were previously considered uncontrollable.
- It reduces chaos. By imposing some structure, you allow for maximum collaboration and coordination while ensuring that people stay in their lanes. It's clear who the point person is. Much like how a beehive operates, everyone knows their job and performs it.
- It supports better decision-making and communication.
- It helps to steady emotions and decrease stress for individual leaders and their teams.
- It helps leaders get info at a time when paralyzing fear stifles information flow.
- It gives leaders the ability to filter out unnecessary or unhelpful information (while retaining accuracy, of course), and react in a thoughtful, reasoned way when it's most difficult to do so.

As you begin putting your plan together it may help to break it down into these five components:

1. Rapid Response Team: a pre-determined group assembled to coordinate actions.
2. Leader in Charge: The central leader or coordinator in charge.
3. Command Center and Alert Code: a predetermined location (physical and/or virtual) for monitoring and reacting to events and a code to let people know assembly is needed.
4. Information gathering.
5. Promote a unifying message.

Let's explore each one in more detail.

Rapid Response Team

The idea here is to put together a team that ensures all relevant key functions, subject matter experts, and decision makers are represented. You'll want to include all senior leaders and leaders of key functions such as operations/logistics, security, finance, HR, communications/PR, facilities, etc. Appoint people to this team before a crisis happens and make sure they know their respective roles and responsibilities. Conduct drills with a variety of scenarios to ensure that all who participate are trained, know what is expected of them, and comfortable with the processes.

Leader in Charge

You really need a central commander. This individual is appointed to manage response activities such as assigning personnel, deploying equipment, obtaining additional resources, and coordinating with participating partners or external agencies as needed. Often, the leader in charge is the senior-most person in the organization. (You will likely need to tap a "second in command" in case the first choice is out of the office, unavailable, or incapacitated when a crisis occurs.)

This leader will want to delegate emergency management responsibilities to other specialists on the team as needed so that he or she can maintain necessary focus on the overall picture of the disaster or crisis.

Strong leaders are always important but in times of trauma they are especially vital. People are scared. They don't know what to do. They look for leaders not only to tell them the next step, but also to reassure them. It takes a team to manage a crisis, but someone needs to keep the team calm, focused, and motivated.

In the heat of crisis this leader should be fully present, visible, available. He or she must be out front showing empathy, listening, and sharing clear and consistent messages so that everyone is on the same page. In chapter 7 we'll discuss ways to "bake in" leader visibility by embracing some proven communication tools. But for now, let's talk about the leader persona that needs to emerge in times of crisis.

The leader in charge must "stand in" unflinchingly and without hesitation in the face of chaos and adversity. This may mean being the protector or defender, shielding others from fallout as much as possible. He or she must lead with calmness and resolve, doing and being what is called for, even when blaming or hiding feels easier. Especially then.

Each team inside departments and units also need a leader front and center, visibly and overtly, to assume the role of point person and to ensure unity for their departments when confusion and fear threaten to unravel the organization. Whatever unit or department you're leading, you can stand in for your group.

Command Center and Alert Code

A command center or operations center is a predetermined location known to all. It's a physical or virtual location from which the rapid response team runs its operations. It should be sequestered (away from the chaos), large enough to house the entire team, be readily available for meeting, have good resources necessary for communicating, and possibly have breakout rooms for teams to meet if necessary. It's also important to pre-identify a back-up location in the event that the default location is inaccessible or destroyed during the trauma.

Your team should select a code word or phrase that puts all these plans in motion. (Some organizations use "Code Rapid Response" or "Code Blue" as theirs; Diana mentioned hospitals tend to use "Code Triage" to assemble their disaster teams.) This allows everyone to go into action immediately, with little explanation. (Remember, time is usually critical at this juncture.) When the code word is used, this is an immediate signal that you have pulled the cord and that everyone should get into position immediately.

Information Gathering

In a crisis situation it's critical to centralize information, facts, and data. You'll need a process for seeking, capturing, sorting out, and disseminating key information. What's known? What isn't known? What's relevant and (just as important) what isn't? Who will serve as trusted advisors? The goal of all of this is organize and coordinate response activities, ensuring that the most pressing needs are met, and that resources are allocated without duplication or waste.

Promote a Unifying Message

A big part of this plan is shaping and disseminating the right messaging. It is vital to deliberately emphasize unity. Remember, when disruption strikes, the shared experience draws people together. This is a manifestation of the fourth F—friend—response. If we jump in right away with a solid communication plan we can capitalize on the "all in it together" camaraderie. This helps people transcend divisiveness.

By working to galvanize and unify the team we give people a way to preserve both self and organization simultaneously. We show them through our words and actions that they belong to something bigger than themselves and need to function as a cohesive, interconnected, interdependent group. The actions of one can have a domino effect on many others, often unseen. There may be individual heroic acts, but to survive and thrive in the aftermath of trauma requires the whole team.

This boils down to purposely ensuring there's not division. There are various ways to do this. We can use bonding/team building activities to enhance a collective sense of belonging. We can firmly and publicly address divisive behaviors like blaming, shaming, and guilting. We can share stories of heroism, goodwill, and camaraderie. And in the aftermath, we can give people meaningful projects to do, like fundraising for a cause or group connected to the trauma they have experienced. But the faster we can get started on intentionally unifying people within the organization, the better.

Creating unity, of course, is a function of great leader communication. This is such an important skill that we determined it needed a deep dive. See chapter 7 to learn why great communication is so crucial to creating a strong organization (in good times and bad) and to receive a set of guidelines to help you create your communications plan.

MAKING THE RAPID RESPONSE PROCESS WORK

As you put together your own Rapid Response Process, you'll want to keep it simple enough that it seems doable, but detailed enough that it is effective. This will take some trial and error. That's fine. No one gets it right on the first iteration. In fact, that's why it's so important to both practice in advance and to conduct an After Action Review after a trauma has occurred.

Once you have a basic plan in place you will find that it's adaptable and scalable. Any type of business can use it and it can be customized for crises and change events of various intensities. You'll be able to train people in it and practice it by "pulling the cord" from time to time so everyone can get familiar with how it works.

A few tips:

- Include the RRP in the orientation process for all new employees. Make sure they're fully aware of the plan and what they specifically need to do in an emergency, as well as what the Rapid Response Team will be doing.
- Keep members of Rapid Response Team sharp. Have them present at orientation for new members. Call them together when major updates occur to the plan, when facility layout or roles change, and so forth. Hold an annual tabletop drill, ideally based on the scenarios in emergency plan.
- Practice makes perfect. Periodically go over the rapid response process so it is fresh in the minds of employees and leaders and to remind them of its value should a traumatic crisis occur. The key is to hardwire emergency concepts and implement basic training of them in advance. Practice organization-wide drills at least annually that include physical assembly of the RRT. This will instill muscle memory. You'll know what to do automatically the next time there is a crisis.
- Don't wait for catastrophe to "pull the cord" by sounding the alarm with your code word. If a situation is at all

worrisome, pull everyone into a room and invoke the Rapid Response Process, even if it ends up being no longer needed and disbanded within a short time. Often you're able to say, "crisis averted" and all is well. But simply reminding people that you have a go-to process in place creates a sense of security and confidence.

Finally, be aware that even with good prior training, when a real event occurs, initially, chaos and confusion will be present. This is especially true when there are more unknowns than knowns. The Rapid Response Process will reduce uncertainty and help to contain the situation, but it cannot and will not eliminate the human factor. Give yourself and your employees some grace and don't expect perfection. In traumatic times—in fact, at all times—we must simply do the best we can.

CHAPTER 7

WHAT GREAT COMMUNICATION LOOKS LIKE IN TIMES OF TRAUMA (AND WHY IT MATTERS)

COMMUNICATION IS A vital leadership competency. This is true in good times and in hard times. When the economy is strong, business is good, and money is flowing, great communication from leaders accelerates performance, strengthens employee relationships, and in general creates a high-performing culture. In times of trauma, it can save your company.

As we discussed in the last chapter, leaders need to be fully present and available in crisis situations. A big part of this is sharing accurate, timely information and giving clear directives. Great communication minimizes confusion and uncertainty, which is often the root cause of anxiety and fear.

Employees need frequent, real-time, transparent communication even when life is relatively normal (if there is such a thing). But in times of crisis and rapid change, this level of communication is even more important. It helps them understand the external environment, which creates a sense of shared urgency. They'll understand the reasons why you're asking them to do things differently, and when people understand why, they're more likely to comply.

What's more, when we communicate well in times of crisis, we can actually deepen trust and confidence in leadership (or perhaps establish it for the first time). Even more important, we create a sense of hope for the future. This hope, underpinned by a vision of the future they can see and buy into, is what keeps people going through some incredibly tough times.

Yet despite how important communication is, many leaders don't realize their skills in this area need work. They often assume they've communicated clearly and with enough information. This is rarely the case. Communication is not just about checking off the boxes ("I sent out a memo about that! What more do they want?") It's not even just about making sure people understand what you say. It's about making sure they engage emotionally with your message and act on it.

Often leaders think they need to have all the answers, or a perfectly written memo or email before communicating. Again, not true. It's better to communicate quickly and in real time, sharing what you know and assuring people that you'll give more information when you have it.

As you can see, we absolutely need to train our leaders in communication, as well as in other leadership skills. Investing in leadership is what allows us to create a high-performing culture that's aligned, adaptive, and nimble. It's what inspires people to take ownership all the way to the front lines, so that things move quickly and consistently in times of crisis.

Organizations need to get deliberate and intentional about communication—both *how* they communicate and *what* they communicate—and make it a priority. This means hardwiring your messaging and cascading it through every level of leadership. The key for ensuring communication is to bake it into your operations in the good times so that leaders will do it in the hard times, almost without thinking.

Typically, we find the problem isn't that leaders make bad communication decisions. It's that they don't plan ahead and are left scrambling, which is made all the more difficult when the leader is under extreme duress or has been traumatized. This often means communication comes too little and too late. And if there's no plan in place that forces regular communication, it almost certainly drops off the radar or becomes problematic when things get stressful. Getting a communication framework in place prevents this from happening.

HOW BAKING IN GREAT COMMUNICATION HELPS COMPANIES

In good times *and* bad, putting a system in place to ensure that leader communication happens regularly, consistently, and effectively benefits companies in many ways. For example:

- **It creates alignment and consistency.** When everyone hears the same messages at the same time, people are motivated to respond in consistent ways. Everyone knows the rules. Everyone works toward the same goals. People in different parts of the company are having similar employee experiences, which in turn means customers get a consistent experience.
- **It leads to better, faster, more efficient execution.** With consistent communication from leaders, people in all sectors understand what they're supposed to do. They are able to act in a coordinated and collaborative fashion to meet clearly defined goals.
- **It prevents people from assuming the worst.** In the absence of clear communication, a void opens up. People don't generally fill voids with positive narratives. They go into guessing mode and jump to conclusions, which often veer far from the truth. This happens in good times too, but when people are in survival mode they're especially susceptible to fear-based assumptions. A strong leader

communication system prevents the void from happening in the first place.

- **It reduces anxiety.** Uncertainty makes people anxious. Telling them the truth (even when it's a truth they don't want to hear) reduces the anxiety that comes from being in the dark.

- **It helps them understand the "why" behind decisions (which, in turn, creates a sense of urgency).** Transparent communication makes people more likely to embrace needed changes. When you say "Here's what's happening and here's how we need to respond," employees feel the same sense of urgency leaders do. This is a big piece of the buy-in puzzle.

- **It creates a culture that attracts and keeps high performers.** When leaders are great communicators who don't hide motives and hold critical information close to the vest, people feel respected and valued. They are expected to jump in and give feedback and solve problems. This is the kind of culture that creates a sense of unity, engagement, and ownership.

All of these factors together create an organization that consistently performs well. In normal times you'll be ahead of the game. In times of trauma you'll be able to leverage your communication system in a way that will increase the organization's likelihood of surviving—and hopefully, coming out stronger on the other side.

THE FIVE <u>VITAL</u> TENETS OF COMMUNICATING IN TIMES OF TRAUMA

As we will discuss momentarily, not everyone will leverage the same communication tools as they implement their communication plan. And of course—as is true with all of the best practices in our road map—your plan will not always look like someone else's. Every company and every traumatic situation is different.

However, to help you get your hands around this step, we have outlined a set of tenets to guide you. We've given them the acronym VITAL, for Visible, "In It Together," Transparent, Accessible, and Listening. Use it as framework for remembering the key elements of communicating in times of crisis.

When you keep these tenets in mind in all communications, you'll be able to reduce chaos, ambiguity, and uncertainty—and build camaraderie, steadiness, reliability, teamwork, and coordination.

Visible

- In times of crisis, it's vital that leaders are highly visible and take the lead on communicating. (As we discussed in chapter 6, this is a pivotal part of "Standing In.")
- Don't hide behind a spokesperson. It's okay to delegate the communication function in the incident command structure, but don't hide behind the spokesperson. Make sure the message comes from you as the leader or incident commander.
- Communication must occur as quickly as possible, even if you don't yet have all the information. Communicate what is known, but also clarify what isn't yet known. *"Here's what we don't know yet. We will share it with the organization as soon as we do know."*
- This doesn't mean overwhelming people with everything there is to say. People don't have the bandwidth to process it all. Figure out what info is essential and share that.
- Communication from leaders must be clear to reduce ambiguity and confusion. Be as simple and straightforward as possible. Be careful not to send mixed messages.

- Be consistent. Establish regular frequency for updates and communicate the schedule so people know when to "tune in."
- Communicate at the unit level as well (in addition to, and even in the absence of, communication that comes from the c-suite level). Senior person in unit communicates department-specific information, conveys information from above, and collects information from those in the workgroup to pass up as needed.

In It Together

- It is so important to always link communication back to your mission, vision, and values. As you set goals, share updates, and communicate wins, always do it within the framework of where you are going as an organization. (This provides a sense of stability when everything is shifting and helps people maintain a sense of meaning and purpose.)
- Convey unity, hope, and the belief that coming together in response ensures better outcome in both the short- and long-term.
- Double down on messages that connect to teambuilding, camaraderie, and purpose.
- Empathy is critical. Encouragement and positivity are important, but resist telling people to get over it or "buck up." Seek to understand how people are feeling without judgment or criticism. Let them know you understand their perspective.
- Messaging that "we're all in it together" also allows for acknowledgment of people's fears, worries, and anxieties as expected and normal. It's fine for leaders to calmly express their own fears as well. This conveys a sense of authenticity and humility.

- Inform people what to expect. Share which processes have been established or will be established.
- Resist all temptation to blame or finger-point, to create an "us vs. them" mentality. If you see this happening, firmly denounce it.

Transparent

- Make sure senior leadership is aligned in how they see the external environment and that everyone agrees on what success looks like. And make sure managers at other levels share the same perceptions. (This is critical to creating transparency and making sure messages are cascaded consistently.)
- Help all employees understand the external environment. People may not always know what's going on. Don't assume that they do.
- Don't create voids with silence or waiting to communicate. If you sense a void exists, move to fill it immediately.
- Tackle rumors head on. Seek out "elephants in the room" and address them head on. For example, call out any fears about the future that you know or even suspect people are feeling.
- Don't withhold information unnecessarily or assume people already know what's happening. In times of survival people assume the worst.
- Don't downplay or mislead. Don't hide financial realities or bad news. Employees are adults and can handle the truth.
- Share bad news the minute you have it. Knowing what's happening is always better than not knowing. This kind of news (losses, layoffs, etc.) must come from the CEO. You cannot delegate it.

- Don't be afraid to say, "I don't know," but follow up with how you'll find out and when you'll convey the answer to them.
- Don't assume silence means no one's talking or concerned.
- Say *why* something is being done, not just what's being done. Everyone deserves to know the *why* behind a decision.
- Clarify that transparent doesn't mean revealing confidential or private information. Be discerning and hold boundaries without being mysterious or coy.
- Make sure all managers are prepared to answer tough questions.

Accessible

- Use all modalities (video, email, intranet, text, in-person town hall and in-person on units if these can be done safely) to convey messages from the senior leader. When it's not possible to be visible in person, connect employees to senior leaders virtually via livestream.
- Have a central repository/FAQ center where people can get info. (This is usually on the organization's intranet site, but may also be posted on visibility or communication boards located within each department or unit.)
- Establish a central number/site for employees to ask questions in between regular communication sessions. This streamlines the flow of info, ensures consistency, decreases the flurry of calls to departments (security, HR, admin, facilities, etc.), and allows collection of data (types of questions, concerns employees have). Those questions also expose holes in information flow which can be plugged.

- If you haven't held town halls in the past, implement them now. Whether you conduct a town hall virtually or live, this is a great opportunity for the leader to convey confidence and provide information, as well as to show humility, impart gratitude, and convey a sense of openness.
- Let people know where they can go to get individualized help. Also, convey that stress and feelings of anxiety are understandable. Do everything you can to reduce the stigma of seeking help when it is needed.
- Emphasize your open-door policy if you have one. Make sure people know you and other leaders are available for one-on-one conversations if an employee has a concern.

////////

A FEW TIPS FOR EFFECTIVE TOWN HALLS

» Set the tone by offering up a warm greeting and giving people a chance to settle in.
» Explain the reason for the meeting and set expectations for the group at the beginning of the meeting. For example, tell people that questions are welcome. However, if there are lots of comments by audience, you may limit each person to a few minutes so everyone gets a chance to talk or ask questions if needed.
» Let others talk without interruption, but politely intervene if it goes too long.
» If the leader has other members of their cabinet in the audience, take the opportunity to direct questions to them as appropriate. But don't "dump" on them. For instance, if an HR question arises, it's fine to refer it to the CHRO, but if it's a complaint or heated, take it yourself first before asking the CHRO to add more detail.

» Know when to move the conversation or question offline. Do not get into a debate or come across as defensive or lashing back.

» Record the Town Hall for others and/or transcribe and send information out. This way those who didn't attend can still get the information and see the questions that were asked.

Listening

This is the fifth letter in the acronym, but it's actually the most important piece of the communication formula!

- Ask questions and leave room for inquiry.
- When listening, stop talking.
- Resist the temptation to just listen for what you want to hear. It's easy to echo all good news, and/or avoid bad news, but your job is to hear and deal with the hard stuff too.
- If you hear a criticism (overt or implied) or tough feedback, don't immediately jump to defend yourself. It is hard to keep listening in these circumstances, but this is where it really counts.
- Acknowledge what you hear—pain, fear, anger, anxiety—without diminishing or dismissing it.
- There is often wisdom in the resistance, a reason behind even the most hostile question. Try to understand where people are coming from. What can you learn from this pushback? Could you be wrong? Are you missing something? Is there a better way?
- Realize, too, that if you have all the answers, then you probably aren't asking enough questions. No leader can

know everything even in normal times. This is especially true in crisis times. Similarly, if it's too quiet, this may be a sign that people feel uncomfortable asking questions. Bottom line in both cases: Ask more questions about how they are doing, what concerns they have, what they are experiencing or observing, and *listen* to the answers.

As you sit down to create your communication plan, keep in mind that no two companies' plans will look the same. There are no hard-and-fast rules on what kinds of tools to use and how often. Many organizations rely heavily on town halls and staff meetings. Others prefer high-tech options like intranet, video messages, and emails. Still others use in-person tactics like rounding (where leaders regularly touch base one-on-one with employees and questions designed to get specific feedback) or daily huddles (where staff gather at a prearranged time to receive information from leaders and share their own feedback).

One commonality is the information cascade. Cascading is critical because only a tiny fraction of the organization reports to the CEO. Basically, each senior leader cascades to their leaders, who cascade to their leaders, and so forth . . . until it ends up with frontline team members.

In normal times you might cascade information every month. In times of trauma you probably need to push out talking points much more frequently—several times a day at the beginning and likely every day thereafter. You might also hold regular meetings where department leaders talk to their leaders about the cascade and about questions that have arisen during department meetings or rounding. This is how you cascade information upward.

Communication should ebb and flow in terms of frequency and method depending on your circumstances. Accelerate and decelerate as needed (think about what makes sense at the moment).

Try out different tools and see what works. The most important thing is to make communication a priority and get a system in place to make sure it happens. When you realize how VITAL "baked in" communication is to creating strong, high performing company—in good times and in hard times—you will wonder how you ever got along without it.

CHAPTER 8

STABILIZING YOUR ORGANIZATION

ONCE THE IMMEDIATE crisis has passed—you've ensured everyone's safety, put steps in place for the future, gotten leaders aligned in their messaging, etc.—your work is not done. Trauma is outside the norm and this phase, moving into stability, is when trouble often arises.

At this point, it's important not to fall prey to hubris ("We've got this under control!") or resort to the stiff upper lip approach ("Stop whining! We've just got to tough this out!"). Also, we need to be careful not let the traumatic event become taboo. Most companies need help facilitating this part because the whole subject is so emotionally charged.

It's here where many companies drop the ball. Some semblance of normal life returns, work gets busy, and it feels like there is no more time to spend on the trauma. But if you stop now, the impact of your initial hard work will be lost.

By leaning into the next three tactics—Conducting a Look Back, Seeking Outside Help, and Naming the Trauma—you'll go a long way toward making sure the healing process that you've already established keeps going.

CONDUCTING A LOOK BACK

What is a Look Back? Some people call it an After Action Review, or AAR. Essentially, it's a structured review or debriefing process for analyzing what happened, why it happened, and how it can be handled better in the future. A Look Back should be conducted immediately following a crisis to chronologically recap the event; elicit feedback, observations, and perspectives from the larger group; and identify gaps in protocol or lapses in performance.

Ultimately, the goal is to generate a comprehensive list of lessons learned. The Look Back gets to the heart of what happened and why. It captures the organization's successes and failures regarding how it handled the crisis. Done well, this increases transparency, bolsters teamwork, and creates a culture of continuous improvement. But be careful: Done poorly, it can result in more blame and finger-pointing.

It's vital to make the Look Back a priority. Quite often leaders are so focused on moving forward that they don't take the opportunity to formally review what went well and what didn't. Admittedly, looking back takes a lot of discipline, and it's understandable that many leaders are reluctant to it. Not only are they exhausted and overwhelmed, they often have an "It's in the past so why dwell on it?" mentality. The problem is, the longer you wait after the trauma begins to resolve, the fuzzier the key details become.

In fact, you might want to do a quick, COVID-19 pandemic Look Back right now. Carefully analyze the immediate safety/containment response your organization implemented in the early days of the pandemic. Identify specific actions. What went well and why? What did not go so well? Identify specific outcomes and behaviors. Capture unexpected dilemmas that arose and clarify processes to use in future crises. Let's say an employee had to make a worker's comp claim from being injured "on the job" at home. How was this handled? How might it be better handled next time?

As much as you can, follow the "how-to" guidelines on the next page. You may not be able to answer all of these questions. For instance, you probably didn't have a Rapid Response Team in place before the pandemic started. That's okay. The purpose of this exercise is to give you a feel for how the Look Back works. In future crises, after you've created your roadmap, you'll be able to answer them more thoroughly.

How To Hold a Look Back

First, assemble a Look Back Team. This is typically comprised of senior leadership and the "section leaders" of those involved in the Rapid Response Team. Call everyone together and explain what you are doing and why.

Keep it simple. Have a facilitator and a record-keeper. Ideally use a flip chart so that everyone can follow along during the process.

Be sure to establish ground rules for meeting. For example, everyone has opportunity to speak. Only one person speaks at a time. No finger-pointing or blaming.

Upfront, emphasize that everyone needs to be brutally honest and transparent about where the failures were as you do this hindsight evaluation. (Sidenote: People must need to feel psychologically safe to tell the truth. If they don't, you've got a serious cultural issue to address.)

Lay the groundwork that it's expected that there will be lots of different points of view, lots of emotion, lots of different opinions around what happened and why. Assert that it is important that the full picture is captured and all perspectives are accounted for.

Here are some questions to ask:

- What went well and why? What were our strengths? Where did we shine? Be as specific as possible.
- What were our weaknesses? Where was there confusion? What went wrong and why? Be as specific as possible. Were processes not followed? Why? (For example, did people not know what to do? Were they overwhelmed with fear or chaos? Were they unaware of safety plans, processes, policies?)
- What things happened that weren't covered by an existing policy or process (in other words, gaps in planning)?
- What conflicts arose?
- What issues arose with convening the Rapid Response Team? Were there delays in alerting/calling for the assembly? Were there logistical issues? Was it clear how decisions were being made?
- What issues arose in communicating what was happening to the broader organization? Were they timely? Were there delays? Was there difficulty in getting the messages out?
- Was it difficult to get information as the situation evolved?
- What questions remain?

Make sure the Look Back session is well-documented. Create a summary with actions to be taken to improve, by whom, and by when.

Leaders are typically conditioned to focus on the future. It can go against our grain to look at the past. But only when we look back can we see where our weaknesses and shortcomings are. It's the only way we can improve and grow as we move forward.

And it's the only way we can get a handle on where we need the expertise and support of others . . . which happens to be the next part of the roadmap we're creating.

SEEKING OUTSIDE HELP

Few companies have the expertise needed to survive a trauma and come out stronger on the other side. They need outside support to help the company and employees function better. The problem is that most leaders are so busy working *in* their business that they don't have time to work *on* their business. Generally, our shortfalls and weak points kind of get ignored or glossed over. We just keep steamrolling on, compensating for our weaknesses as best as we can as we make the most of our strengths.

But when trauma, crisis, or major change happens, suddenly these weaknesses are exposed. We're navigating new territory and we don't always have the knowledge and skills we need to find our way. Plus, leaders and employees alike are often traumatized. It suddenly becomes obvious that we need outside help. If we haven't planned for this moment it can be hard to know where to turn in the heat of crisis.

That's why *right now* is the time to start compiling a guidebook/library of resources. Don't think because you made it through one crisis that you're okay and will just know what to do next time. First of all, consequences may still be unfolding. Second, the next crisis that hits might be worse. Third, you shouldn't accept just "scraping by" as good enough. This is a chance to get stronger and better.

We view seeking help as a two-pronged endeavor. Prong one is *logistical*. Here we're talking about the stuff you need to keep the business running smoothly, keep customers satisfied, etc. Prong two is *psychological*. Very often after a trauma people will need help processing intense emotions. Let's talk about these one at a time.

The Logistical Prong

Here you will identify gaps in your internal expertise. Again, you might want to use your experience with the pandemic as a jumping off point. What weaknesses did this recent crisis unearth? Do you need updated technology? Better logistics? Supply chain enhancements? Do you need help with media relations? A better security system? Extra legal support? Do employees need regular COVID-19 testing?

If you did the COVID-19 Look Back we just described it may have identified some gaps, but feel free to add to that list.

Slowly start taking steps to shore up these gaps. Rome wasn't built in a day, but get started sooner rather than later. Put together a schedule and put some deadlines in place. If you don't get things on the calendar they won't happen.

The Psychological Prong

Outside help is often needed for a traumatic event to be fully processed. It's important to a) know the "red flags" to look for that show people may be traumatizead and b) make sure people can get the help they need.

It's especially important to get outside help if leaders are impacted by traumatic events. Their emotional health impacts their behavior which impacts everyone else, so if they have an issue it can have a big impact on the organization.

We urge you to revisit chapter 3 to review signs and symptoms of trauma. For example, if people are refusing to change, lashing out angrily, or exhibiting a marked change in personality (such as suddenly going silent), they may well need counseling or some other form of mental health assistance.

Be especially mindful of people who were "close to the action" during a trauma—meaning those who may have witnessed an act of violence or who may be especially close to someone who was directly involved. And pay special attention if a trauma is an ongoing one that will involve a long investigation or end in criminal charges or termination for those involved.

Ensure that people are able to get the psychological support they need. Some organizations have robust Employee Assistance Programs (EAPs), peer-to-peer support groups, and access to one-on-one counseling. If yours is one of them, make sure people know these services are available. Even if a formal EAP is not in place in your organization, it's still important to urge people to seek mental health support when they need it.

Do all that you can to de-stigmatize the need for mental health support. Go out of your way to assure leaders and employees that getting help isn't a weakness. Rather, it's a way to strengthen yourself, your team, and the entire organization.

NAMING THE TRAUMA

"Nothing can be changed until it is faced."
JAMES BALDWIN

When an organization goes through trauma, it's critical to call it what it is. Depending upon the kind of trauma or severe crisis you've experienced, it may not be hard to name it. For example, it's usually not difficult or upsetting to refer to a minor earthquake, or a traffic accident. But trauma that has resulted in death, loss of life or job, or other kind of major disruption or destruction—and where there is significant blame, shame, and guilt—is harder to name.

Struggling to call a trauma by its name is a pattern that occurs in many organizations. One trauma that is difficult to name is sexual assault. It can be hard for people to say, "We have had a sexual assault in this organization," or "A person committed sexual assault." Because it is hard to use these strong words or labels, people may tend to use softer words, like "the incident" or "that thing that happened."

After the shooting at Memorial Hospital, Diana and her colleagues were reluctant to say the words "the shooting." When they did reference it, some used "4/16," the date of the shooting, as shorthand (much in the way we use "9/11"). While this lessened the blow, some people found it offensive or overly dramatic.

Why We Struggle to Name Trauma . . .

There are many reasons people shy away from naming trauma. In the case of the shooting it was a loaded conversation on lots of levels. There were strong beliefs around why it happened (some people wanted someone to be "responsible") and many employees felt uncomfortable pointing the finger. Also, there was a belief that people should just get over it and move on, and thus it didn't need to be talked about. Diana reports that sometimes people would avoid the topic because they didn't want to upset her or remind her of the event.

It's true that talking about trauma is triggering for some people. But a bigger truth is that for almost everyone the subject is just uncomfortable. It is difficult to talk about the grief and loss associated with trauma. In general, our society isn't comfortable with difficult topics. (You may have noticed that people say someone has "the big C" or whispers the word *cancer.*) We don't really know how to bear witness. We don't have the words. And many of us desperately want to avoid our own discomfort with someone else's pain and grief.

Plus the blame, guilt, or shame usually associated with the trauma makes it really hard to talk about it. This is especially if an insider caused the trauma (not a common enemy) and/or if there is moral injury. Naming exposes these tendencies of blame, shame, and guilt as expected emotions. It reminds us that there are many points of view, that we don't have all the information or facts, that we have our own histories with the others involved (perpetrators or victims). It shines a light on our own beliefs about why bad things happen, and that we create a narrative to make sense of the situation or have an answer. These are all tough topics to talk about . . . and so we don't.

. . . And Why We Must Name It

It's really this simple: If we don't openly address the traumatic event it cannot be emotionally processed and the organization cannot heal. People will continue to struggle and the ongoing, perhaps deepening polarization, blame, shame, and guilt will hurt the culture of the organization. This damages trust, camaraderie, belief in one another, collaboration, cooperation, cohesiveness, teamwork, and so forth.

In a preview video on the website for the Collective Trauma Summit 2020, Psychiatrist Dan Siegel notes that "Collective trauma becomes intensified when it's ignored."[1] He says this in an interview focused on race relations, but the same holds true for any kind of trauma. If we don't talk about it, hear one another's perspectives, and empathize with their experiences, we can't heal from it. This is a good lesson for organizations.

George Santayana said, "Those who forget the past are condemned to repeat it." We would modify that to, "Those who deny and avoid dealing with a trauma are condemned to have even more difficulty getting through a crisis in the future."

The How of Naming (What Can We Do?)

So how do we name trauma? The most important action we can take is to talk openly and as often as needed. Discussion helps to normalize individuals' reactions to trauma and organizational patterns that arise. It allows us to accept that survival mode, initially, is to be expected—and also makes it clear that we don't have to be held hostage by it.

Being open about the subject will reduce the likelihood that it becomes taboo, off-limits, too difficult to talk about, or unspeakable. It will increase organization-wide dialogue and learning, decrease division, and strengthen relationships.

If trauma has resulted in, or has potential to lead to, deep division, or if it is extremely emotionally loaded, you may need outside help. An expert can help you craft an approach and strategy to naming your trauma and facilitating discussions about it.

Rituals can also help. For example, if someone has died by violence you might hold an annual memorial service. This shows that it's okay to talk about the event and it also helps people process residual grief.

If a traumatic crisis had a massive impact on business you might hold a celebration when goals are met or metrics improve. Part of that ceremony would include talking about the event and how far you've come. Again, this shows that the event is okay to talk about and it goes a long way toward proving that the organization hasn't been limited by it and isn't defined by it.

Hopefully, the three tactics we have just explored will help you shore yourself up during the stability phase. In the next chapter we'll discuss what we're calling the "Long View" portion of our road map: integrating the traumatic experience in meaningful ways, and seizing the opportunity to build our team into one that's stronger, better, and more openminded and unified than it was before.

CHAPTER 9

ORGANIZATIONAL LONG VIEW: HARDWIRING PREPAREDNESS

A S WE ESTABLISHED on the first page of this book, we live in a time of constant change. Only organizations that can bend and flex with the wind will survive long term. But there is no short-term fix for becoming that kind of company. You have to put the right systems and process in place. And you have to figure out a way to make them stick.

The reality is that preparedness is hard. We make all these big changes and for a while we follow them. In the beginning we think we've got it all figured out. We're excited about the new way of doing things. But over time we begin to slip. Little by little our new practices drop off. New pressures present themselves. Old leaders leave and new ones replace them.

Before we know it we're back to where we started. We've poured all this time, effort, and money into being change ready and one day we realize we've let it slip through our hands.

The bottom line is that we have to find a way to hardwire all of our hard work. We have to create an organization whose processes and structures allow us to keep operating in perpetuity—an organization that doesn't revolve around a single person or depend on superstars.

One of the few good things about trauma is that it exposes our weaknesses. It becomes an opportunity to redesign ourselves so that we get stronger and better than before. It allows us to transform so that we don't have to settle for surviving. We can thrive.

Deep meaning often comes out of trauma. There's that initial sense of camaraderie, that "we're all in it together" moment, that occurs before we divide apart. We have the opportunity to say "Wait a minute, let's really capitalize on the part where we did come together. Let's really capitalize on our purpose and our mission."

A TIME OF RETHINKING

Trauma can be a wake-up call not just for individuals but for the organization. It's an opportunity to get some clarity around what we do, how we contribute and add value, and why we're unique in providing these services. Instead of just reacting we can choose to get very intentional about the things we do. We have the chance to take a step back and ask: *Is the business no longer able to offer some of the services it had in the past? Has trauma actually created new opportunities? Given what has happened, has our mission changed in any way?*

Typically, while the services a company offers *do* change after a trauma, our reason for being often doesn't. We are often inspired to reaffirm our collective purpose and realign each team and individual to that. Leaders get clear on our *why*—meaning why we lead at all, and why we lead inside this organization.

During the reestablishing phase, silver linings may emerge. We realize that yes, a bad thing happened, but we're able to take inventory of the things we learned, the good things that emerged, and where we performed well and why. Often our attention is drawn to people's ingenuity, bravery, selflessness, or quick thinking.

Sometimes we realize that a process in place did work as planned. Some of these things will have been identified in our Look Back, but we need to be highlight them as the company comes together to look toward the future.

BUILDING STRONGER, BETTER TEAMS

A trauma is an opportunity to review how the team has functioned, to honestly reflect on what has been working well and what has not. This is the time to ask, "What did we observe during this crisis? What are the strengths and weaknesses in our team? What gaps do we have in expertise, experience, temperament, and creativity? Where do we need to fill those gaps, either internally or otherwise? And how do we re-bond as a team, and move forward?"

Here are a few recommendations:

- Discuss your aspirations for the team: What's the ideal way to work together?
- Ask "What values are posted on our wall? And do we really live those values?" Most companies claim values like trust, respect, integrity, authenticity. Discuss them. Are they more than just words? Do we all define them in the same way? Do we truly live them? What's missing?
- Develop a set of guiding principles for the team. Set some ground rules for productive interaction and for navigating conflict, disagreements, and breakdowns in communication. Put practices in place to decrease internal toxic competition. Establish openness to others' ideas—avoiding echo chamber, megaphone, or cancel culture dynamics—and encourage high-quality critique, tolerance for dissension, and debate.

- Create a team vision statement. For example, Diana shares this one, developed following the shooting at the hospitals she served as:

> "We are a team that, as a whole, is greater than the sum of our parts. We are a team in which the very best of each is shared, the very best of each is nurtured and the very best of each is expected. Each of us fully embraces the responsibility and the privilege of stewardship and courageous leadership, and our actions reflect the values of accountability, best practices, compassion, and synergy. We are a team whose talents and strengths are fully expressed and whose members are deeply connected to the mission and the legacy of the organization. We know and believe that what we do, and who we are, makes a profound difference in the lives of others."

- Establish ongoing team-building activities to create connectedness and a sense of belonging.
- Conduct training at all levels of the organization in skills designed to maximize teamwork: focusing on skills like meeting facilitation, conflict resolution, resilience, and so forth.
- Discuss what's in place for developing, mentoring, and sponsoring up-and-comer leaders. (Some organizations already have leadership development programs, but many may not. This is too important an area to leave to chance.)
- Establish succession planning as an ongoing process, not as episodic.

REINVENTING HOW WE MAKE DECISIONS

As we mentioned before, trauma has a way of exposing flaws in how decisions are made. Some organizations may be slow and bureaucratic. Others may have a top-down structure in which decisions are made quickly, but people complain that few others get any input. Take time to explore your flaws and finally take steps to mitigate them.

In most organizations, decision-making doesn't occur via a formal process. Most leaders can't really articulate how it's done. When pressed to describe it they tend to bring out the organizational chart to show who has authority over functions. But an organization chart is an insufficient illustration: decision-making is about more than authority or identifying who is in charge, it's a process and a philosophy. Organizations that don't take the time to clearly define how decisions are made typically struggle to achieve great (and sustainable) outcomes.

The good news is you can create a decision-making process that is a force multiplier. The process can be both speedy *and* high quality, efficient *and* agile, innovative *and* consistent, dynamic *and* stable, and take into account short-term needs *and* the long view. And you can create a process that generates decisions that are superior to ones made by any one person alone.

You may think you don't have time to redesign your decision-making process. In reality, you don't have time not to. The ability to implement better decision-making allows your business to be faster and more agile, to decrease frustration, to have the right people around the table, to gain better insight, to communicate more easily, to get more buy-in . . . and to do less undoing of decisions made poorly.

Here are a few recommendations:

- Visually map your current decision-making processes to affirm the essential steps, identify temporal requirements, and expose the flaws and bottlenecks.
- Determine goals and desired outcomes of your decision-making process. You may want decisions that leverage both sides of the polarity pairings. Here's an example of some decision-making principles grounded in polarity thinking:

> We follow rigorous, well-defined processes when making decisions *and* our decision-making process is adaptable enough to handle the various issues we face.

> People advocate for what they believe in *and* they are curious about what others think.

> We are able to maintain objectivity when making difficult decisions *and* we demonstrate concern and compassion for others when making decisions.

> We act quickly and decisively when making decisions *and* our decisions are fully informed by having the right people involved (e.g., subject matter experts, people with the authority to decide, stakeholders).

> We are resolute in, and committed to, our decisions *and* we are willing to revisit our decisions when new information emerges.

- After talking about the goals of the model, assess the kinds of topics, issues, and projects that typically came to leadership for problem-solving or approval. Group them into major categories (e.g., capital equipment purchases, construction projects, operations, contracting for outside services, employee engagement/benefits, etc.)

- Consider flipping the model: Rather than having a single executive team meeting to discuss and make decisions on a wide variety of unrelated topics, consider establishing separate decision-making committees, each specifically focused on one of the major categories you've identified (e.g., capital equipment, construction, contracting, etc.). In addition to populating the committees with senior leaders, add subject matter experts (e.g., finance, facility, and IT experts to the capital purchase committee) to round out the expertise.
- Create a standard agenda format. For example, it may include the reason for a topic being brought forward, the time allotted for it, and the desired outcome (e.g., for information, for approval, for discussion and input).
- Establish a standard presentation template that identifies the minimum info/data required, and any pre-signoffs that may be needed (e.g., from facilities or IT) before coming to committee.
- Establish ground rules for committee meetings. For example, include guidelines around how conflicts will be resolved and whether decisions will be made by consensus, vote, majority, chair or single authority, etc. The method may vary, but must be declared up front so that all know for each topic how the final decision will be made. Be sure to define what "consensus" means so that all are on the same page. Consider appointing a "devil's advocate" to argue unpopular viewpoints so you can make sure all sides of an issue are thoroughly explored.
- Create a P&P to describe your decision-making philosophy and process. This will help everyone in the organization to know how decisions are made. Consider creating a visual to illustrate the committee structure and the flow/ steps required for approval. This can be used to orient new

leaders and share with members of the organization at large with the goal that everyone knows "how decisions are made around here."

- Review the process periodically for opportunities to improve it.
- Establish methods for communicating major decisions to the organization as a whole (e.g., town halls, posting on intranet, announcements) and make it a regular practice to keep people in the loop. Make sure to say "why" a decision has been made (and "what's in it for them" if appropriate). All of this reinforces trust and creates confidence that leaders are transparent and on top of things.

//////////

A NOTE ON PROBLEM SOLVING

Typically, when we are solving problems in groups, people jump quickly to solutions. They may take sides and vociferously advocate for (and get attached to) "their" solution. (Often because there's a polarity involved!) They get into a battle to win. Here's a better way:

First, clearly identify the problem, with facts, data, objective and subjective impacts. Explore why it's a problem and how big a problem it is. It's surprising how often we begin solving a problem without clearly defining it.

Articulate the goal. What is the ideal outcome if we solve this problem?

Declare how the final decision will be made. Will it be group consensus? Vote? Discretion of the senior-most leader? Or is the group making a recommendation to another decision-making body? The point is to make it clear to participants what happens with their decision or recommendation.

Identify all possible (reasonable) solutions, including doing nothing. With each, list the pros and cons. Lay out how you'll mitigate the cons if you choose that solution. Identify additional stakeholders to consult with as needed.

Then, debate and discuss and come to a decision in the way that you've previously defined.

///////////

CHANGE IS THE SINGLE CONSTANT

Nothing is permanent. That's one of the big life lessons reinforced by trauma. Once we experience one kind of crisis we realize that another crisis can (and probably will) happen again. Change is constant and relentless. We must always be ready for what it brings.

Part of hardwiring preparedness is realizing the process is far bigger than you or any one leader. Earlier we mentioned succession planning is no longer episodic, but ongoing. It used to be common for a CEO to stay for twenty years. When they left, everything got reinvented. Now, with leaders coming and going far more frequently, this system no longer makes sense. The decision-making model can't depend on one person. You can't lose ground when a CEO is leaving, wait for the new leader to come in reinvent everything, and then rise again.

When a new leader comes in, yes, you still get to capitalize on their energy and vision, their enthusiasm, their style, and the experience they bring with them. But when you have a solid structure hardwired in place your ability to operate isn't put on hold until that new leader gets up and running. You're not doing that rise and fall. You're able to keep moving.

It's this agility, this adaptability, this ability to bend and flex with the (hurricane force) winds of change rather than being flattened by them that's the real payoff of the crisis roadmap we've laid out in these pages. We've given you some guidelines, but only you can put in the work.

When we face traumatic crisis (and plain-old change) head-on and intentionally navigate through it, we become better, stronger, wiser, braver, more innovative, and more effective than we were before. This is true of individuals and it's true of organizations. Let's move from trauma to triumph together . . . and let's get started now.

NOTES

Introduction

* Anjali Sundaram, "Yelp Data Shows 60% of Business Closures Due to the Coronavirus Pandemic Are Now Permanent," CNBC, September 16, 2020. Accessed at https://www.cnbc.com/2020/09/16/yelp-data-shows-60percent-of-business-closures-due-to-the-coronavirus-pandemic-are-now-permanent.html.

Chapter 1

* "How to Manage Trauma," National Council for Behavioral Health, infographic, n.d. Accessed at https://www.thenationalcouncil.org/wp-content/uploads/2013/05/Trauma-infographic.pdf?daf=375ateTbd56.

Chapter 6

* "Evacuation Plans and Procedures eTool," United States Department of Labor, Occupational Safety and Health Administration. Accessed at https://www.osha.gov/SLTC/etools/evacuation/checklists/eap.html.

Chapter 8

* "The Power of Collective Healing," The Collective Trauma Summit 2020 website. Accessed at https://collectivetraumasummit.com/.

ABOUT THE AUTHORS

MARK GOULSTON, MD, FAPA

Dr. Mark Goulston is a board-certified psychiatrist, fellow of the American Psychiatric Association, former assistant clinical professor of psychiatry at UCLA-NPI, and a former FBI and police hostage-negotiation trainer. He is the creator of the Theory Y Executive Coaching that he provides to CEOs, presidents, founders, and entrepreneurs, and is a TEDx and international keynote speaker.

He hosts the *My Wakeup Call* podcast, where he speaks with influencers about their purpose in life and the wakeup calls that led them there, and is the cocreator and moderator of the multi-honored documentary *Stay Alive: An Intimate Conversation about Suicide Prevention.*

He appears frequently as a human psychology and behavior expert across all media, including CNN, ABC/NBC/CBS/BBC News, *Today, Oprah, New York Times, Wall Street Journal, Forbes, Fortune, Harvard Business Review, Business Insider, Fast Company,* Huffington Post, and Westwood One, and was featured in the PBS special *Just Listen.*

He is the author or principal author of seven prior books, including *PTSD for Dummies, Get Out of Your Own Way: Overcoming Self-Defeating Behavior, Just Listen: Discover the Secret to Getting Through to Absolutely Anyone, Real Influence: Persuade Without Pushing and Gain Without Giving In,* and *Talking to Crazy: How to Deal with the Irrational and Impossible People in Your Life.*

DIANA HENDEL, PHARMD

Dr. Diana Hendel is an executive coach and leadership consultant, former hospital CEO, and the author of *Responsible: A Memoir*, a riveting and deeply personal account of leading during and through the aftermath of a deadly workplace trauma. She and co-author Dr. Mark Goulston also recently collaborated to author *Why Cope When You Can Heal?: How Healthcare Heroes of COVID-19 Can Recover From PTSD*.

As the CEO of Long Beach Memorial Medical Center and Miller Children's and Women's Hospital, Hendel led one of the largest acute-care, trauma, and teaching hospital complexes on the West Coast. She has served in leadership roles in numerous community organizations and professional associations, including as chair of the California Children's Hospital Association, executive committee member of the Hospital Association of Southern California, vice chair of the Southern California Leadership Council, chair of the Greater Long Beach Chamber of Commerce, board member of the California Society of Healthsystem Pharmacists, and leader-in-residence of the Ukleja Center for Ethical Leadership at California State University, Long Beach.

She earned a BS in biological sciences from UC Irvine and a doctor of pharmacy degree from UC San Francisco. She has spoken about healthcare and leadership at regional and national conferences, and at TEDx SoCal on the topic of "Childhood Obesity: Small Steps, Big Change."